What Leaders Are Saying

"*The Windshield Is Bigger Than the Rearview Mirror* is an outstanding, uplifting book! With humorous anecdotes and wise insight, Dr. Wickwire inspires us to embrace the hope found in our God-ordained vision and to release everything that lies behind that might hinder our pressing on to His perfect plan."

John Bevere, author; speaker; president,
Messenger International

"What an incredible job Jeff Wickwire has done in explaining things we already knew but probably had not pondered why. Progress is often connected to your vision. This book is eye training for travel. It will keep your eyes focused on the road—on your destiny, on Him. Thank you, Jeff Wickwire, for sharing your life, character and even a problem or two with the rest of us. Pardon me while I adjust my rearview mirror and set my cruise control."

The **Rev. Tommy Tenney**, GodChasers.Network

"Getting stuck in the past is one of the most common battles that Christians face—and the enemy revels in it because it distracts us from God's plan. I can assure you that at one point or another, this book will give you or a friend fresh vision. Jeff Wickwire provides clear biblical and present-day examples to show how living in the past keeps us from fulfilling God's call and purpose. I am confident that he will help readers move on and discover the joy that awaits them on the other side."

James Robison, president and founder,
LIFE Outreach International

"This book is a must-read for those attempting to make the most out of their 'messes'! In fact, there is a miracle in your mess, if only you'll look for it. Pastor Jeff Wickwire's insights give us practical keys to divine encounters yet to come, and he does a splendid job of helping us learn from the past without letting it rule our present."

Bishop Harry R. Jackson Jr., author; speaker; senior pastor, Hope Christian Church

The Windshield Is Bigger Than the Rearview Mirror

CHANGING YOUR FOCUS FROM PAST TO PROMISE

Jeff Wickwire

Chosen
Grand Rapids, Michigan

Published by Chosen Books
a division of Baker Publishing Group
P.O. Box 6287, Grand Rapids, MI 49516–6287
www.chosenbooks.com

Printed in the United States of America

Library of Congress Cataloging-in-Publication Data

Wickwire, Jeff.
The windshield is bigger than the rearview mirror : changing your focus from past to promise / Jeff Wickwire.
p. cm.
ISBN 0-8007-9404-4 (pbk.)
1. Christian life. I. Title.
BV4501.3.W535 2006
248.4—dc22 2005022685

I dedicate this book to the two greatest kids God ever gave to a dad. To Jeremy, for his intelligence, creativity and all-around good heart. And to Julia, for her ceaseless caring for the hurting of our world, and for her beautiful smile. You have both made me very proud!

Contents

Foreword by Tommy Tenney 9
Acknowledgment 11
Introduction 13

Part 1 The View through the Rearview Mirror
1. Hooked on the Past 17
2. The Longer You Linger 31
3. Those *Weren't* the Days 45
4. Lost Love's Lure 59
5. Failure's Frightening Face 75
6. Tied to a Trauma 89
7. Bitten by Bitterness 105

Part 2 The View through the Windshield
8. Has Anyone Told You It's Over? 121
9. Crossings 135
10. On the Other Side 149
11. Your Greatest Potential 163
12. True Treasure 177

Foreword

There is a reason why windshields are bigger than rearview mirrors. Cars were never meant to be driven backwards. Propping your arm on the backseat—contorting your neck, head and shoulders to drive looking backwards—is, needless to say, an awkward position. Everything in a car faces forward. Forward movement is the intentional design of an automobile.

If man knows how to engineer a car to go forward, God knows how to engineer humanity to move toward Him. Everything about us is meant to look forward—toward Him. In order to look behind us, we virtually have to turn around—and turn our backs to Him.

What an incredible job Jeff Wickwire has done in explaining things we already knew but probably had not pondered why. Progress is often connected to your vision. This book is eye training for travel. It will keep your eyes focused on the road—on your destiny, on Him. An occasional glance back is not only permissible, it is often helpful. Just remember, though, you were never intended to stare with regret at the things behind you that can never be retrieved. Your faith pushes you forward.

Thank you, Jeff Wickwire, for sharing your life, character and even a problem or two with the rest of us. Pardon me while I adjust my rearview mirror and set my cruise control.

Jeff Wickwire is a man who does not quit. You cannot be afraid of failure and start three churches. You cannot give up easily and start three churches. You cannot live your life looking behind you and create an effective ministry for the future. From searing success to heart-wrenching failures and betrayals, Jeff Wickwire's ministry has spanned the seasons of life. How he learned to move on down the road is explained in this book in clear automotive but spiritual terms. The windshield *is* bigger than the rearview mirror—and there is a reason for it!

The Reverend Tommy Tenney
GodChasers.Network

Acknowledgment

The Scriptures spoke truly when declaring, "Who can find a virtuous wife? For her worth is far above rubies" (Proverbs 31:10). Throughout the many testings of time and circumstance, much is revealed, one thing being what those around you are really made of. My wife, Cathy, has proven to be that ruby of surpassing value. Having been with me for more than half my life, she has proven out yet another observation of the wise King Solomon: "The heart of her husband safely trusts her. . . . She does him good and not evil all the days of her life" (verses 11–12). I could not have written this book without her undying belief in God's calling on my life, and her endless encouragement when the infamous "writer's cramp" paid its predictable visit. It humbles me to know that I have no greater fan in my court.

Introduction

In A.D. 79, the ancient city of Pompeii was transformed instantly into a graveyard of ashes when Mount Vesuvius erupted, raining fire and brimstone onto the unsuspecting inhabitants. One of the more chilling archaeological finds of the eighteenth century was the uncovering of these ruins, revealing thousands of people frozen in time. They are lying in beds, sitting in chairs and curled up in streets, holding hands, their faces recording terror.

To the modern observer, the occupants of Pompeii seem locked forever in a moment from which they cannot escape. Time passes around them—seasons come and go, new generations learn of their uncanny fate—but still they seem to live in that instant of their destruction, forever halted from moving forward into the next day of their lives. This was not a choice that they made—to be locked in the past. But many of us, amazingly, do choose to do just that: We cannot look beyond the decision or event or catastrophe that keeps us in the past and hinders every day of the future. Is this your current condition? Do you feel chained to the past? If so, you *do* have a choice. You need not remain frozen in a moment or season during which you were hurt, disillusioned, offended or shattered. You can move on!

One of the most sinister thieves of a joyful, fulfilling life is what I call "rearview mirror" focus, looking backward to a past of pain, regret, would have been's, could have been's and should have been's that rob us of present happiness and future promise. Countless thousands live in the shadow land of painful memories or inordinate attachments to a person, place or thing that has long since passed in the night.

If this describes you, this book is dedicated to helping you gain freedom from the past. The God who loves you deeply is longing to step into your pain and turn it around. As we begin our journey, I urge you to consider the words of Isaiah the prophet, for they sum up the focus of this book beautifully: "Do not remember the former things, nor consider the things of old. Behold, I will do a new thing, now it shall spring forth; shall you not know it? I will even make a road in the wilderness and rivers in the desert" (43:18–19). Do you already feel a stirring of hope? So do I. Let's begin!

Part 1

The View through the Rearview Mirror

Do not say, "Why were the former days better than these?"
For you do not inquire wisely concerning this.

Ecclesiastes 7:10

You can clutch the past so tightly to your chest that it leaves your arms too full to embrace the present.

Jan Glidewell

Hooked on the Past

"Escape for your life! Do not look behind you."
Genesis 19:17

Nostalgia is a seductive liar.
George W. Ball

We love the past . . . ever noticed that? Our society is rife with nostalgia, with everything from proliferating "Golden Oldies" radio stations to brand-new magazines like *Reminisce*, which promises its readers "memories from a simpler time." It seems that everywhere we look we are lured into romance with yesteryear. Many of Hollywood's blockbusters strike gold by turning a wistful eye to the past—films like the historic tragedy *Titanic*, which delves into the lost love of an aged woman, and *Cocoon*, which reveals the longing for recaptured youth. Another favorite film, *Somewhere in Time*, tells of the beauty and mystery of finding true love by being

We should all have "stones of remembrance," memory markers that remind us of the times when God moved mightily on our behalf.

supernaturally transported into the past. Oh, yes, we are fascinated with *then*.

Now, there is nothing in the world wrong with looking back and appreciating a fascinating slice of history or with casting a longing backward glance to a time when no nuclear threat, AIDS, air pollution or terrorism loomed over us. It is only natural to recount times when God has been good to us in days gone by. The Bible reveals, in fact, that He regularly instructed His people to do so. Christ Himself left for the Church, as an act of remembrance, the practice of partaking of the Lord's table. Paul wrote about this in 1 Corinthians 11:26: "For as often as you eat this bread and drink this cup, you proclaim the Lord's death *till He comes*" (emphasis added). Those final three words leave no doubt that we are to "look back" at what Christ accomplished for us on the cross and celebrate it until He reappears in the clouds at the dawn of a new age (see Matthew 24:30 and 1 Thessalonians 4:17).

We can trace this act of remembering back to the early days of Israel's history. After striking the firstborn of Egypt with judgment and "passing over" the people of Israel, for instance, God told Moses, "So this day shall be to you a memorial; and you shall keep it as a feast to the LORD throughout your generations. You shall keep it as a feast by an everlasting ordinance" (Exodus 12:14). To this day, the Jewish people look back to the Passover and honor it, just as God commanded.

After Moses' death and upon Israel's first trek into the Promised Land, God gave specific instructions to Joshua (Moses' newly appointed successor): "Take for yourselves twelve stones from here, out of the midst of the Jordan, from the place where the priests' feet stood firm" (Joshua

4:3). Joshua later instructed the twelve men who had been chosen to represent each tribe:

> "Cross over before the ark of the LORD your God into the midst of the Jordan, and each one of you take up a stone on his shoulder . . . that this may be a sign among you when your children ask in time to come, saying, 'What do these stones mean to you?' Then you shall answer them that the waters of the Jordan were cut off before the ark of the covenant of the LORD. . . . And these stones shall be for a memorial to the children of Israel forever."
>
> verses 5–7

God clearly wanted the future generations of Israel to look back to the past in order to build their faith.

In these biblical cases, the past events served as "stones of remembrance," memory markers that reminded God's people of the times when He moved mightily on their behalf. Following this biblical example, we should all have "stones of remembrance," recalling times that God led us forward in His blessings.

And along with the successes in our journeys, the past can also serve as a solemn reminder of hard-learned lessons, ones that, if we remember them, can prevent us from repeating the same costly errors. Contrary to the prevalent belief that we do not learn from the past, *we should and can learn every valuable lesson God sends our way.* The apostle Paul painstakingly rehearsed the sins committed by the children of Israel in the wilderness, stating that "all these things happened to them as examples—as object lessons to us—to warn us against doing the same things; they were written down so that we could read about them and learn from them in these last days as the world nears its end" (1 Corinthians 10:11, TLB). When we read of Israel's idolatry, sexual sins, and complaining and murmuring, we must learn from her past errors and avoid falling into the same traps today.

These biblical stories (and others) illustrate the healthy, beneficial practice of looking back. We can recall past blessings of God in order to strengthen our faith, and we can remember our past sins (apart from experiencing condemnation and tormenting guilt) to gain wisdom for the future.

So when is assessing the past counterproductive and even destructive? At what point does looking through the rearview mirror become a drag on our faith and a hindrance to our lives? It is when ghosts from the past paralyze us and render us incapable of moving into the future. *When something "back there" holds us—this reveals the need for deliverance.* For all such "prisoners" the past is not a pleasant or productive place.

I do not dispute the fact that we sometimes need to assess the past in order to understand ourselves better. Brief glances into the rearview mirror are beneficial to gaining perspective, but that is not my focus in this book. Think a moment. Have you ever known someone (maybe yourself?) who constantly looked back to an unresolved offense? Or who was trapped by self-inflicted unforgiveness due to a personal failure? Perhaps the death of a loved one, an untimely decision or a failed business venture caused discouragement and fear of moving forward. Maybe a haunting personal trauma, such as sexual abuse, or a broken love relationship left a shattered heart in its wake.

If you are pondering whether or not having an excessive focus on the past is really all that important, let me assure you that the answer is yes! An unhealthy fixation on the past can and will rob you of your future. Throughout Part 1 of this book, in the next six chapters, we will explore six "chains" our adversary uses to hold us "back there" in hopes that we will spend today stuck in yesteryear. These chains are:

- Inordinate attachments to someone or something
- Past successes

- Heartbreak
- Failure
- Trauma
- Bitterness

Those trapped in the past are robbed of joy, achievement, meaning and God's best until they are set free. All hope of forward movement is lost. Rather than the past being a place they occasionally visit, those who fall prey to these triggers make the past their home. Yesterday becomes their jailer, captor, tyrant and ultimate reality.

Later, in Part 2, we will shift our sights to the exciting future that waits for you. God has a plan older than earth itself. You don't discover it; He discloses it. The destiny that He has in store is one of the most compelling reasons to shed any unnatural, drawn-out attachment to the past. So, let's move on and explore some of the chains that can bind us *back there*.

Are You Chained to Your Past?

How can you know when a chain holds you to your past in an unhealthy way? What is the difference between glancing in the rearview mirror for perspective and focusing on the past to the extent that it requires healing and deliverance? Here are a few warning flags:

1. You are preoccupied excessively with an event or events, a person or people.
2. You are unable to let go of a past event, even in spite of your best efforts.
3. You long excessively for a past time or place.
4. Vivid, recurring memories conjure fear, guilt, anger or bitterness.
5. You have the prevailing belief that "those were the days" and there will never be any that are better.

Do any of these ring a bell? I tell you, Jesus came to set us free from traps like these! Because they are traps with spiritual roots, only one thing will remove them—God's truth. We are affected by what we experience, but we are changed by what we know. Jesus said, "And you shall *know* the truth, and the truth shall make you free" (John 8:32, emphasis added). The less we know of God's Word, the more susceptible we become to the traps and snares laid by the enemy of our souls.

We are going to discover that the chains noted above are part and parcel of Satan's arsenal against God's children and must be defeated by spiritual weaponry. "The weapons we fight with are not the weapons of the world. On the contrary, they have divine power to demolish strongholds" (2 Corinthians 10:4, NIV). *The New Strong's Expanded Exhaustive Concordance of the Bible* (Nelson, 2001) explains that the English word *stronghold* is taken from a Greek word meaning "to fortify, to hold safely." A stronghold refers to something that holds you securely in its grip; a stronghold "holds you strongly." It carries the idea of a well-fortified castle in which the bound are held captive.

In context, Paul is speaking of thoughts that exalt themselves against God's will. "We destroy false arguments; we pull down every proud obstacle that is raised against the knowledge of God" (verses 4–5, GNT). That is exactly what the chains that bind us to the past seek to accomplish. Satan does not want you to have "knowledge of God" as it relates to His purposes for you. So he baits your mind with thoughts, reasoning and arguments that rise up against God's will and declare defiantly, "This child of God will be bound to the past. He or she will not walk in the fullness of God's plan!"

Think about it. If the fish displayed on that plaque in the fisherman's lodge could talk, he would probably say, "If only I had known what lurked behind that harmless-looking worm! It all happened so fast. At first, an appealing meal appeared before my eyes . . . *Chomp!* Then out of nowhere I felt a sharp stab and a tug—what was going on? Next,

Behind every spiritual battle is a devil that does not want you to discover the blessings God has in store for you.

I felt a long, barely visible line pulling me against my will. Before I knew it a frightening being held me in his clutches and, well, the rest is history." The worm was the lure that led the unsuspecting fish to a surprise demise—much like the bait of Satan.

Know for certain that Satan is behind this plan for our demise, and if he can he will use an unhealthy obsession with the past to lure us ultimately into his "boat." He will do anything he can to conceal the wonderful future God has in store for us. He loathes the thought of your catching a glimpse of what waits on the other side of your decision to be freed from bondages of the past. Hear me well: *The enemy does not want you to enter into the fullness of God's plan for your life.* He will do anything to stop that from happening. In light of this, let's begin to view Satan as the great illusionist; the evil being that he truly is.

I remember vividly watching a scene in an old Hercules movie when I was a boy. Hercules (played by Steve Reeves) was captured by the enemy and placed at the bottom of a slave ship. After shackling his legs to the deck, a ruthless guard cracked a whip over his head repeatedly and shouted, "Row! Row! Row!" Of course, as the story told it, all of that rowing eventually developed Hercules' muscles to the point where he was able to break free. But the point is, that scene reminds me of how Satan cracks the whip of idolatrous emotional attachments, past successes, heartbreak, failure, trauma and bitterness to remind us relentlessly of the pain and grief of yesterday when we should be focused on tomorrow.

The Bible's Hall of Famers

I have been encouraged to find that some of the Bible's greatest heroes could have easily been derailed from their purpose if they had gotten stuck in the past. Take, for instance, Paul and Moses. It is hard to imagine that Paul, the writer of two-thirds of the New Testament, did such horrible things prior to his conversion. We first encounter him as Saul before the dramatic changes in his life. The future apostle to the Gentiles was a willing witness at the martyrdom of Stephen. You may recall that Stephen was stoned to death—a miserable and cruel way to die. The Bible says that "the witnesses laid aside their robes at the feet of a young man named Saul" (Acts 7:58, NASB).

Saul wreaked havoc in the Church, "entering every house, and dragging off men and women, committing them to prison" (Acts 8:3). He later admitted, "I persecuted this Way to the death. . . . Also when they were being put to death I cast my vote against them" (Acts 22:4; 26:10, NASB). The mighty apostle, who was so capable of leading converts into a confession of Christ as Lord, had once "compelled [believers] to blaspheme; and [was] exceedingly enraged against them" (26:11). Paul openly confessed that he "persecuted the church of God beyond measure" (Galatians 1:13).

Moses, the mighty deliverer, leader, lawgiver and prophet of Israel, also had a past. When he was around forty years old (see Acts 7:23), he spied an Israelite being beaten by an Egyptian. He had already made up his mind not to be called the son of Pharaoh's daughter (see Hebrews 11:24–26) and began to identify himself with God's enslaved people. Thinking that no one was watching, he killed the Egyptian in cold blood and buried the corpse in the sand. The following day he attempted to act as a peacemaker between two Hebrews, but soon became aware that his murderous deed was known. He quickly fled to Midian, where he would spend the next forty years in hiding as a fugitive.

The guilt over what these two future world shakers had done must have presented a formidable battle for each of them! No doubt, the vicious accuser of the brethren fired his red-hot arrows of condemnation deep into their hearts. The very name *devil* comes from the Greek word *diabolos*. The prefix *dia* means "through"; *bolos* comes from a word that means "to throw." When you put the two words together you discover a being that hurls accusations forcefully with the intent of piercing or going through his victims. Our archenemy's forte is to blast us with fiery darts that carry this message: "You're not good enough. God would have used you if you hadn't done this or gone there or said that. Now, it's too late. You're finished! God can't use you anymore." This is the standard fare of a condemning devil. In spite of this, Moses and Paul overcame their guilt and went on to become mighty movers and shakers for God!

My Call out of the Past

You might think that it was different for Paul and Moses, great men of God, real Hall of Famers. You might think that they had some special dispensation to hurl the effects of the past over their shoulders and fulfill their callings. So I want to share with you a personal experience, a story from the perspective of a "regular person" just like you.

One night during the height of what has been tagged the "Jesus movement," I was sitting in a home Bible study that I had recently begun attending. I was eighteen years old at the time and was fairly fresh out of the hippie movement. About two years before, while I was in a juvenile home on a drug charge, Jesus had touched my heart. All I knew was that He was suddenly real to me, and that I loved Him very much. It happened as a minister was teaching. He quoted a verse out of the Song of Solomon and at that moment it felt as if the verse grew wings and flew straight into my heart, carrying with it a red-hot coal. I became aware immediately of an unexplainable desire to speak His Word. I can only explain it as an "urgent urge to utter." It was incredible! As time passed this desire only grew, and though I had come from a troubled past, no amount of denial or resistance on my part could quench it.

The God of the Bible, our God, has the unmistakable ability to transform hearts. His calling often manifests in the form of supernatural desire. No, it is not difficult to discover your calling. What do you really desire to do? What moves you and brings fulfillment to your soul? Pay close attention to supernatural desire. If the things that move you line up with Scripture, you are probably well on the way to discovering what God wants you to do! Your heart can be likened to the burning bush that greeted Moses on the day God called him to deliver Israel from bondage: "And the Angel of the LORD appeared to him in a flame of fire from the midst of a bush. So he looked, and behold, the bush was burning with fire, but the bush was not consumed" (Exodus 3:2). The bush burned, but the fire did not destroy it because it was a holy fire—the supernatural presence of God that transforms every yielded heart. (We will explore this in greater depth in chapter 6.)

The burning bush is a perfect picture of good heartburn—and that is what I experienced in the Bible study. All who receive this touch are consumed with an overwhelming urge to do whatever God has called them to do. This was true of Jesus, of whom it was said, "My devotion to your house, O God, burns in me like a fire" (John 2:17, GNT). The prophet Jeremiah was similarly captured by a desire from which he could not escape: "His word was in my heart like a burning fire shut up in my bones; I was weary of holding it back, and I could not" (Jeremiah 20:9).

Looking back, I know there was yet another reason why this new desire in me had to be supernatural. Of anyone I knew, I was the least likely to stand in front of people and say anything. I had terrible stage fright! It all began with a play when I was in the sixth grade. It was one of those class projects, with the desks reconfigured to give more space and everyone given a part. My part was to come walking into my classroom from the hall, clad in a cardboard suit of armor, and deliver a few lines. On cue I clunked in, stood in position and went completely blank. My mind became an empty screen. The heat of embarrassment rushed into my face as my classmates began to snicker and then laugh. Mercifully, the teacher excused me from the room. As I went clunking back out into the hall, the following words flashed like a neon sign across my mind: *You are not cut out to be in front of people.*

The seed was sown, and, unfortunately, future experiences only reinforced this belief. Whenever I was asked to say something at a Christmas gathering, birthday party or any other social function, my lower lip would tremble, my mind would draw a blank and the same red-hot rush of embarrassment would flush my face. Each time a little voice would repeat the old mantra: *You are not cut out to be in front of people.*

Despite this deep-seated insecurity, God proved that He had begun a new work in my heart. Unable to escape the growing desire to declare His Word, I began to pray for an opportunity to speak. Keep in mind that at this time in my life I still had hair down to my shoulders, weighed 130 pounds soaking wet at six foot one and was only a few years down the road from my juvenile-home salvation experience. I had not completed high school. I was the world's most unlikely candidate for preaching! Still, the deep yearning would not leave me alone. In fact, the more I prayed the worse it got. Then one day my pastor approached me with an opportunity.

"Hey, Jeff, I received a call from a friend of mine," he said. "He needs a guest speaker for this Sunday and you were the first person to come to mind. Can you do it?"

My pastor's words did not have the effect you might think. As soon as I heard him, I was terrified. "Me? Gosh, I'm not sure. Uh, I don't know if I'm ready for that," I muttered, my heart pounding in the heat of fear.

My past, with all its dire pronouncements, was coming into direct conflict with what God was saying *to* me *about* me!

"Well, I told him you would do it, Jeff. I believe this is the Lord," he said with a stern gaze.

I remember saying something like, "Okay, well, I'll go pray about it."

When I walked out of his office, the past rose up like skeletons coming out of graves. *You'll flop!* a little voice said. *You'll make them regret they ever invited you to speak! Don't you remember what happens every time you stand in front of people?* I literally became sick. Unable to eat, sleep or concentrate on much of anything, I felt my future calling to minister His Word clash with ghosts from the past. On two occasions I called my pastor to decline, and both times he told me it was too late and that I would do just fine.

Our past will define us if we let it. Negative experiences can become the hands that mold us, the prophetic voice of what we will become. Through the years I had grown shy, reclusive and totally lacking confidence. My past, with all its dire pronouncements, was spewing arguments into my mind to keep me from accepting what God was saying *to* me *about* me! God was saying, "Stand up. Be bold. I have put My Word in your mouth!" This reminds me of Gideon in Judges 6, whom God called to deliver Israel from the Midianites. The Angel of the Lord came to Gideon suddenly and said, "The Lord is with you, you mighty man of valor!" (verse 12). Gideon was stunned. He responded out of what his past had taught him: "O my Lord, how can I save Israel? Indeed my clan is the weakest in Manasseh, and I am the least in my father's house" (verse 15). God had called Gideon a man of valor at the same time that Gideon's past labeled him as the weakest and the least.

Like Gideon, I had a choice. I could live in the past and allow it to dictate the conditions upon which I would live out my life, or I could walk out of the past and believe what

God was saying about me. Satan was casting his bait. Who would have guessed that behind the lie that I was among the weakest and the least—I was not "cut out" to stand before people—was an invisible line held by an ancient, evil "fisherman" who was hoping that I would take the bait and wind up in his boat of defeat? It is abundantly clear to me now. I was on the verge of discovering my calling, and Satan was doing all he could to stop me.

Against all inner protests, I went and preached that Sunday. It had occurred to me during the week that I had no idea whatsoever how to prepare a message or even how to stand behind a podium and address a crowd. I knew absolutely nothing about how to carry myself properly, make eye contact, use appropriate gestures or anything else that had to do with the mechanics of public speaking. When the associate pastor introduced me, I was dressed in blue jeans and the nicest shirt I could find, and my long hair was pulled back in a ponytail. Yet, in spite of my "insufficiencies," I had received a message from God during prayer—a verse had stood out—and I was determined to stand up and tell the tiny congregation what that verse meant to me.

My memory of that service is a blur. I think I preached for about fifteen minutes, experiencing the strange sensation of watching someone else's mouth talk. I heard my voice, but I could not believe it was actually mine. At the close of my message I gave an invitation. To my astonishment, several people responded and gave their hearts to Christ. Several more came to the altar for prayer. When all was done and I drove away, a wall began to crumble within me. It felt much like the falling of the Berlin Wall, which had liberated so many thousands from the tyranny of Communism. My "wall" had been built on lies from a distant past. The belief that I could not be effective in front of people, and that I was too shy to stand before a crowd, began to be replaced with a newfound boldness. Satan's "chain" of past failure (which I will go into more in chapter 5) could no longer be pulled inside of me, even though he had used it so many times in the past. That very day I stepped out of the shadows of my past into the sunshine of a brand-new future; a destiny Satan had fought hard to prevent me from finding.

We must be delivered of the traps our enemy has used so effectively and grab onto what God is saying about our *future*. Proverbs 29:18 says, "Where there is no vision, the people perish" (KJV). Backward focus always results in frustration, wasted potential and futility—but without fail, forward focus brings purpose, discipline, excitement and much greater meaning and victory to our lives.

With this in mind, let us move forward to explore the first chain that causes us to hang onto the old and stale, even when it comes at the expense of discovering something new and fresh. We are about to see that the longer you linger in yesterday, the more you may forfeit tomorrow.

Points to Ponder

1. Since recalling the past can be healthy and beneficial, have you established "stones of remembrance," memory markers that remind you of God's past goodness? List a few "stones" that come to mind.
2. Which chain has Satan pulled successfully to lock you in your past in unhealthy ways? How long has this been going on? Are you ready to do something about it?

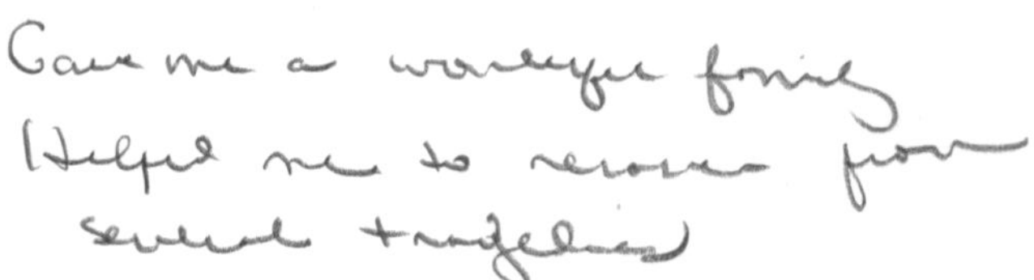

The Longer You Linger

And while he lingered, the men took hold of his hand.

Genesis 19:16

Some people stay so far in the past that the future is gone before they get there.

Anonymous

As the morning sun slowly peeked over the sultry Middle East horizon, an anxious family of four fled the infamous city called Sodom. Two angelic visitors hurried along the man, named Lot, and his wife and two daughters, just before the fiery judgment of God fell. "Escape for your life!" one of them cried (Genesis 19:17). The clock of imminent judgment was ticking. The sins of Sodom and Gomorrah had reached the point of no return. In minutes, the once-grand cities of beauty and commerce would become a heap of smoldering ruins, a grim reminder that God will not be mocked.

Lured by her affections, Lot's wife was paralyzed by what had been instead of what would be.

Then the heavenly messengers gave one final command to the somber family: "Do not look behind you nor stay anywhere in the plain" (verse 17).

Tragically, Lot's wife blew it. She was unable to resist a stolen glance back as the fires of judgment rained down on the city. Scripture records: "But his wife looked back behind him, and she became a pillar of salt" (verse 26). In a nightmarish flash, Lot's wife was transformed into a macabre statue of salt, forever memorialized looking backward, back to a place that God had cursed.

Curiosity was not the only culprit in her tragedy. Her fated glance also revealed the core of her affections. Though God had taken her out of Sodom, the cursed city yet remained in her heart. Lured by her affections, Lot's wife was focused on what had been instead of what would be. This woman's experience is a timeless illustration. Backward focus paralyzed her from being able to embrace the new life that God was bringing.

Lot almost suffered the same fate. The Bible records that earlier, "while he lingered, the men seized him and his wife and his two daughters by the hand" (verse 16, AMP). By lingering, Lot was holding his family on the edge of destruction because his past affections were in a lethal tug-of-war against God's new direction. It was merciful action for the heavenly visitors to pull them out of the city.

The longer we linger in a past God has called dead, the more statue-like we become, and the harder it is to leave. When we remain stuck in the desert of yesterday, we are rendered incapable of moving forward into our purpose. This tendency—to linger back there when we know that we should be moving forward—happens to us all. Heel marks are usually the best indicator that I have been dragged, kicking and screaming, out of the old and into something new. As He did with Lot, there have been times when God had to mercifully "seize" me in order to bring me to a new destination.

The question is, Why do we linger—especially when, like Lot's wife, the place we are being called out of is not fulfilling, and perhaps even painful or destructive? Remember the six chains that our enemy uses against us so skillfully? In this chapter we are going to examine chain number one: Inordinate emotional attachments, either to something or to someone. Here is an important reality in the Christian experience: If need be, God will step into the pains, attachments and whimsical longings that carry us excessively into the past and say (as He did to Lot), "Get up, get out of this place! Do not look behind you or stop anywhere in the valley" (see verses 14 and 17). In essence God was saying, "I am bringing change to your life. It is time to move forward, and I'm not asking for your vote!"

Some of what we cling to can be misleading. That is, the object is not really doing for us what we believe it is. This requires God's merciful hand to remove it and show us otherwise. I once had a pet raccoon named Rascal, after the well-known book. If you know anything about raccoons, you know that they are collectors of all things shiny. If they can get their hands on a coin, a silver bracelet, a Coke-can top, anything that glitters, they will grab it and quickly hide it away. They also wash everything they eat. They will take a chunk of meat in their cute little hands and dip it in a bin of water, swishing it back and forth until they are satisfied it is clean.

One day, in a moment of mischief, I gave Rascal a sugar cube. (I know what you may be thinking: *That was mean*! Believe me, Rascal lived the life of Riley and survived the sugar cube caper quite well. Nevertheless, I did repent.) True to form, he immediately dipped it in his little bowl of water and rubbed it in his hands. You can guess what happened next. To his dismay the cube of sugar disappeared. He made his little chirping noises as he searched in vain through the water for the dissolved cube. What he thought held promise faded away. It was an illusion.

Our enemy specializes in giving us "sugar cubes." We think we have something of value, only to discover later that it sifts through our fingers. Though we may search for it with all our might, we discover with time that it was an illusion. In the beginning it looked right, felt right and seemed right, but it turned out to have no substance. This is quite unlike the blessings of God. Proverbs 10:22 tells us: "The blessing of the LORD makes one rich, and He adds no sorrow with it." The blessings of the Lord are substantive; Satan specializes in the art of making empty promises.

Granted, not everything we attach our hopes to is an illusion. Whether we are lingering over a person, a job or a much-loved hobby, many of the things to which we become attached do indeed bring fulfillment and joy. Some relationships God brings into our lives, for instance, are very real and beneficial. In chapter 4 we will discuss in detail how some people come into our lives for a reason, some for a season and some forever. The key is in learning to discern which is which, and that can be very tricky. But right now we are focusing on attachments that linger beyond the will of God and that will eventually interfere with His purposes for us. This is why we call them inordinate, which means to be excessive or immoderate. Inordinate attachments can chain us to the past and, as with Lot's wife, cause us to linger around danger and destruction.

Jesus referred to the story of Sodom and Gomorrah, encouraging us to "Remember Lot's wife" (Luke 17:32). Why? Because her ability to obey God was ruined by inordinate attachments. Just prior to mentioning her, Jesus warned His followers about the day of His return, comparing it to the vivid destruction of Sodom and Gomorrah:

> Likewise as it was also in the days of Lot: They ate, they drank, they bought, they sold, they planted, they built; but on the day that Lot went out of Sodom it rained fire and brimstone from heaven and destroyed them all.
>
> Luke 17:28–29

Do you catch the picture? Life was going on as usual in the twin cities when sudden judgment fell. Jesus said that His return would happen the same way. Suddenly, unexpectedly, when life is going on as usual . . . He will appear. Then Jesus went on to say: "In that day, he who is on the housetop, and his goods are in the house, let him not come down to take them away. And likewise the one who is in the field, let him not turn back" (verse 31). In other words, we must learn how to keep a loose grip on our stuff! Don't allow excessive attachments to stand in the way of your dedication to Christ! In *Matthew Henry's Commentary* (Zondervan, 1999), the great scholar wrote: "Let them not look back, lest they should be tempted to go back . . . an evidence that the heart was left behind."

Jesus' warning concerning preparedness for His return is also valid for day-to-day Christian living, whether or not we live to see His reappearance. We cannot allow ourselves to hang on to past attachments that keep us from following Him. This is a particularly wily trap of Satan because, in this instance, it is not pain that is keeping us roped to the past, it is something good that keeps us there, something we do not want to lose. The Proverbs warn: "Keep and guard your heart with all vigilance and above all that you guard, for out of it flow the springs of life" (4:23, AMP).

Generally speaking, those who look back constantly do not have much going on now. Lingering is a sure sign that there is a lack of fresh vision. If the past is the best you have at this moment, let me declare to you that God has something better. Lot's wife could not receive the fresh leading of God because she was tied to Sodom and all its memories. Anyone who spends excessive time "looking back" to the object of his or her desire is in danger of becoming a "pillar of salt," a mere form of what used to be. God cannot move us forward into a new day of destiny if we are "looking back."

Under the Hood

One morning while driving our son, Jeremy, to school my wife, Cathy, realized that her vehicle was accelerating each time she removed her foot from the gas pedal. Rather than slow down each time she withdrew her foot, the car would begin going faster. By the time Cathy pulled into the school parking lot to let Jeremy out, the engine was racing wildly. Managing to maneuver the car back onto the street, she felt as if a ghost were pushing the gas pedal down, carrying her helplessly faster and faster. The vehicle seemed to possess a mind of its own. After screeching around corners and racing down side streets, Cathy finally managed to pull over into a vacant lot and bail out after hurriedly putting the "ghost car" into park and shutting off the engine.

Soon a friend arrived on the scene, popped the hood and exclaimed, "Wow! No wonder you couldn't control it!" Inside of the engine, just beneath the air filter, sat a perfectly constructed pack-rat nest—full of dog food!

When I learned of it, I quickly connected the dots, recalling comments I had made to my family one night that our dog sure was eating her food faster than usual! As it turned out a little pack rat, knowing that winter was just around the corner, had been dutifully carrying one chunky piece of dog food at a time from our dog's bowl in the garage, up the car wheel and into the warm engine. That fateful morning one lone piece of dog food had become lodged in just the right place, causing the accelerator to stick. The mystery was solved. An undetected intruder had brought chaos and confusion into our lives.

This is exactly how inordinate attachments operate in us. Every day that we live with inordinate attachments to the past can be likened to the enemy lodging one more chunk of dog food into our "spiritual" engines. Then slowly, incrementally, life becomes unbalanced. Finally, we careen out of control, experiencing the awful feeling of being "driven" by an unwelcome force. Eventually we discover that the "rat" is Satan, and that he has used inordinate affections to drive us into confusion. *Anything* that removes God from center stage will eventually produce chaos and pain. This is why Jesus told us to make seeking the Kingdom of God our number one priority: "Seek first the kingdom of God and His righteousness, and all these things [clothes, food, water, all the necessities of life] shall be added to you" (Matthew 6:33).

The Flip Side

I would be remiss if I neglected to mention that lingering is not always a negative act. Staying in a particular situation can be helpful if done for the right reasons. The virtues of patience and perseverance are highly praised in Scripture. Jesus taught His listeners in Luke 18:1 that "they should always pray and not give up" (NIV). What things are we to "always pray" about? For one thing, I believe we must pray about those things we truly believe are worth staying with or "lingering over" until a breakthrough comes—things like a faltering marriage or perhaps a job that you do not have peace to walk away from. There have been many times when God directed me to remain in something from which my flesh wanted to flee. In those situations, lingering in faith and obedience yielded results that ultimately glorified God.

The apostle Paul told this to the Philippian church:

There are times in our own experiences when there is no longer a redemptive reason for staying, especially when we can hear the voice of God calling, "Come forth!"

> For what is life? To me, it is Christ. Death, then, will bring more. But if by continuing to live I can do more worthwhile work, then I am not sure which I should choose.
>
> Philippians 1:21–22, GNT

Can you sense Paul's dilemma? He was saying that he would rather have gone to heaven to be with Christ than to remain alive on earth. In not too many words, Paul was describing his predicament by stating that he was "caught from both sides." How did this great apostle settle his conflict? *He chose to focus on the needs of others rather than to serve his own desires.* "But for your sake it is much more important that I remain alive. I am sure of this, and so I know that I will . . . *stay on* with you all, to add to your progress and joy in the faith" (verses 24–25, GNT, emphasis added). Paul made the decision to "linger" in order to enhance the spiritual growth of others. We are all the beneficiaries because he did just that.

So the issue of lingering comes down to either *lingering in faith* through obedience to God or *resisting* God due to one of the six deceptive chains of our study—inordinate attachments, past successes, heartbreak, failure, trauma or bitterness. If, like Paul, we linger in a situation for a redeeming, God-glorifying reason, it is a positive decision. But note that even positive lingering can become counterproductive and self-destructive if we allow it. Lazarus, for instance, was in the grave long enough for there to be, according to Martha, a stench (see John 11:39). Likewise, there are times in our own experiences when we are lingering in something that has begun to rot. We have to recognize in such cases there is no longer a redemptive reason for staying, especially when we can hear the voice of God calling, "Come forth!"

The Fine Art of Letting Go

I was once involved in a ministry to which I had become attached, so much so that it had become my "home away from home." In that special place I had first learned to teach the Bible, as well as to lead in praise and worship. All of my good friends were there. To describe it in spiritual terms, I would have to say that it was once an ever-flowing river of life for me. In every service God moved on my soul in a special way—until one day I became aware of the still, small voice of the Holy Spirit speaking deep within me. A restlessness that I could not explain was growing in my heart. It was as if God were saying, "It's time to go." *Go?* I thought. *Why in the world would I want to leave?* Yet, the inner nudge persisted, "Go."

I regret that I did not obey God. Looking back, I know that was one of those instances in which I should have hearkened to the verse that says, "Trust in the LORD with all your heart, and lean not on your own understanding" (Proverbs 3:5). It is our *own understanding* that so often gets us into trouble. For all intents and purposes, something can look right, feel right and seem right, yet according to God's purpose, *it isn't.* As time passed, several of the relationships I had developed began to go sour. The leadership changed and along with it the whole tenor and emphasis of the church services. As it had been with Lazarus, the "corpse" (the old thing God had already called me out of) began to rot. By the time I finally left I wished desperately that I had obeyed sooner. It would have been a much more positive parting.

The past can become an idol when inordinate attachments to something *back there* prevent us from obeying Him *right now.* The past may refer to a person, a job, a house or a town; it can even speak of a memory. I started my first church deep in the heart of East Texas. My family and I lived on four beautiful acres atop a scenic hill that had once been a favored spot for deer hunters. My children were

Never remain in a place where God has already left. Never stay when the presence of the Lord has gone.

being raised in a perfect "Mayberry" environment. There were times that I could not imagine life ever being more ideal. As the years rolled by, seven to be exact, every emotional and sentimental attachment to that season of my life blossomed in my soul. Oh, yes, my first pastorate was a blessed milestone. The relationships we formed were wonderful. Our situation was so ideal I can remember thinking, *I'll retire here.*

Then, as in the ministry I described earlier, God began to "stir my feathers." He wanted us to move to a particular city, and this impression would not leave my spirit. I fought an intense inner battle. Why? You guessed it. I did not want to let go of where I was; there were so many precious memories! For an entire year the tug-of-war raged within me between what I finally realized was an excessive, sentimental attachment and the will of God. Finally, I gave in and moved. Our next church reached thousands for Christ, a greater outreach than we ever could have conceived of in a small country town. That experience taught me *never to remain in a place where God has already left. Never stay when the presence of the Lord has gone.*

The Forgotten Cross

As we have seen, affection toward any person or thing that takes precedence over the Lord must be dealt with. So how do we walk away from attachments that hold us tightly in their grip? Listen closely to what Jesus said:

> "You must put aside your own pleasures and shoulder your cross, and follow me closely. If you insist on saving your life, you will lose it. Only those who throw away their lives for my sake and

for the sake of the Good News will ever know what it means to really live."

Mark 8:34–35, TLB

The cross has one message for our self-driven, willful society: Die so that you can live.

Simply put, *Jesus invites us to die.* In fact, the cross has one message for our self-driven, willful society: *Die so that you can live.*

Consider this: A cross is made of two pieces of wood, one placed horizontally and the other vertically. The two pieces "cross" each other near the halfway point. We could say that the vertical piece points toward heaven, while the other piece follows the horizon of the world. For me, this is a vivid picture of its function. We encounter the cross at the juncture of our decisions, whether they are major or minor. We must decide which way we will go. Will we crucify our flesh and lift our hearts upward toward God's will? Or will we refuse to pick up the cross and choose instead to go the way of our own desires, staying in line with the world?

When we choose to go upward, the Holy Spirit becomes the crucifier: "For if *by the Spirit* you put to death the misdeeds of the body, you will live" (Romans 8:13, NIV, emphasis added). As He guides us through this process, the Spirit of God empowers us to die so that we may experience new life. Paul testified, "I die daily" (1 Corinthians 15:31). There is enduring hope and new strength on the other side of crucifixion! Jesus knew this well: "For he himself endured a cross and thought nothing of its shame because of the joy he knew would follow his suffering" (Hebrews 12:2, PHILLIPS). Do you see that? Jesus faced the cross in Gethsemane before He ever faced it in the physical realm. In other words, He chose to die rather than to save Himself. He knew that resurrection life waited on the other side, and this enabled Him to embrace the process that would release this supernatural power to the world.

The truth being told, though Christians express great affection for the cross, we shun its power in everyday life—

because the cross is hugely intrusive. Think about it. How many times each day do you deal with the cross? Let's say, for instance, that a major business decision presents itself. You could make a lot of money, but in order to do so you must compromise a godly principle. The cross rises within you and says, "Pick me up and die that you may live." How would you deal with this? In a less weighty context, how do you respond while driving in rush-hour traffic when someone nearly runs you off the road and you want to give him or her a "piece of your mind"? The cross rises within you and says, "Bless that person! Die so that you can live." Would you take up your cross and follow Christ?

Rather than viewing the cross as an instrument of pain, may I suggest that you begin viewing it as an enormously protective friend? In reality, the cross protects us from *ourselves.* It keeps the monster called our "flesh" from destroying us. Although our soul is reborn at the point of salvation, we still walk in a "house of flesh," which wars endlessly with the Spirit of God within us. That flesh must be crucified. Paul instructed that "they that are Christ's have crucified the flesh with the affections and lusts" (Galatians 5:24, KJV). Notice the word *affections.* The flesh has *affections* that must be crucified or it will cling to the very thing God wants us to release . . . including everything that would chain you to *back there.*

Are you wondering, *Well then, Jeff, how do I "shoulder my cross"?*

You can apply the cross to areas that need to die in the following ways:

First, *admit that the Holy Spirit is bringing the cross before you concerning a certain area of your life.* For me, it has always been that inner nudge that says: *Jeff, this has to end. It must be dealt with and you must let go. You must die that you may live.* Admitting to the reality of this nudge is half the battle.

Second, *say yes to God.* Jesus taught us to respond by letting our yes be yes (see Matthew 5:37), because whatever goes beyond this is from the evil one. Making the decision to agree with God is crucial to applying the cross.

Third, *repent.* Repentance is a *good thing*. It is the gateway to freedom, the key to liberty. Making the past an idol through lack of repentance is a sin. Believe me, I know. I have done it. According to Strong's *Concordance*, *repent* literally means "to recognize or to change one's mind." When we repent it is the beginning of the end for whatever sin or iniquity has held us captive.

Fourth, *make whatever changes necessary to reinforce your decision.* This may require discarding possessions that hold you to memories. You may also need to stop asking others about things that relate to *back there*. Cut every cord. Do not allow anything into your life that stirs up the old nostalgic emotions. The past is the past because it has *passed*.

Fifth, *surround yourself with people who support your decision.* Do not, and I mean *do not*, allow yourself to be around people who pull you down. If you have been running around with a bunch of nostalgia addicts (like you used to be), say good-bye.

Sixth, *seek God with all your heart and be excited*, because leaving what bound you has positioned you for "a new thing."

Finally, *fill your heart with Scripture*, particularly with verses that pertain directly to your struggle. "The law [Word] of the LORD is perfect, restoring the soul" (Psalm 19:7, NASB).

Once you have taken these steps, let the Holy Spirit do the rest. Each day that passes in obedience to Him means that the chains of the past are loosening their grip. A new day with a new perspective will emerge. Be patient. Though you may experience occasional pangs to return *back there*, they will eventually subside. Your willingness to let go, "wipe the dust off of your feet" and move down the road of your destiny holds great reward!

Now, let's get ready to expose another chain our adversary uses that can be surprising. The reasoning the enemy uses sounds something like this: "Those were the days. Your best days are behind you. Your greatest time of usefulness is over." *The devil is a liar.* Follow me to the next chapter and let's learn why.

Points to Ponder

1. Have you sensed God urging you to release something in your past that Satan has been using as a chain to hold you? Is it a struggle to obey? If so, why?
2. In which areas of your life do you sense God calling you to apply the cross? What is your response to Him at this moment? Can you look beyond the crucifixion of your flesh to see the long-term benefits?

Those *Weren't* the Days

Do not say, "Why were the former days better than these?"

Ecclesiastes 7:10

There has never been an age that did not applaud the past and lament the present.

Lillian Eichler Watson

"Nostalgia is like a grammar lesson . . . you find the present tense and the past perfect." So gushes *Reminisce*, the fast-growing magazine I mentioned earlier that is dedicated to the sweet memories of yesterday . . . but was the past really perfect? Is that why we long for it? The very definition of *nostalgia* in Webster's *Dictionary* expresses the fleeting nature of the past: "a wistful or excessively sentimental yearning for return to some past period or irrecoverable condition." Note the words *irrecoverable condition*. Try as we might, we cannot return to the past!

We paint yesterday with a fresh coat of misty-eyed emotionalism, not remembering that when we were there we were wishing for better days.

But still we try, and past successes become another powerful tool of the devil. The notion of the "good old days" is all about mentally recapturing a slice of time that is no longer available to us. This whimsical phrase carries with it the idea of those magical moments when it seemed that love grew effortlessly, success came easily, laughter rose frequently and life always went our way. As a popular song intoned, "Those were the days, my friend."

Have you noticed, though, that we are all too easily inclined to glorify the past when, in fact, we did not feel that way at the time? We paint yesterday with a fresh coat of misty-eyed emotionalism, not remembering that when we were there we were wishing for better days. Do you remember complaining *back then* about the way things were? Do you remember that *even then* you had problems, secretly wishing things could be different? Your answer should be a resounding yes! Yet, we romanticize what *was*, and by doing so, we malign what *is* today. It has been said that nothing promotes the "good old days" more than a poor memory. Oh, there is such truth in that statement!

Think of another popular song, this one by the Beatles. "Yesterday" nicely captures the notion of romanticizing the past. Did you sing along about believing in yesterday? This song was written to a hauntingly beautiful melody, but while we listen we must beware—this is not a healthy philosophy to live by; in fact, it is a delusion. Think about it. Did "all your troubles" really seem to be so far away back then? This is how we sugarcoat the past, especially when things are not going so well in the present.

Does this strike a chord with you? Does your life seem dismal right now in comparison to the glories of the past? Perhaps your responsibilities have multiplied. Maybe an unexpected heartbreak has left you reeling. Or you lost a job . . . your spouse walked out . . . something has gone wrong with the kids.

You might feel as though you are in a pressure cooker. A persistent knot could be gripping your stomach. You could be older, grayer and feel as though you do not have the *joie de vivre* you once did. A slow-rising panic could be gripping your soul as you wonder, *Are the good times really over?* The thought of never again hitting a homerun could be plaguing you, and though it is hard to believe, fear can have a louder voice than faith.

Here is a word of warning: If you are leaning on feelings, they will not hold you up. As a result, you will not be as confident, strong or capable as you could be. In other words, focusing on "knocking the ball out of the park" in days gone by can cramp your ability to believe it can happen again. I think that this is one of the reasons Solomon warns in Ecclesiastes 7:10 to avoid asking why "the former days [were] better than these." Implied in that question is a huge dose of doubt and insecurity: I can't do it again. Nothing good can happen to me now. I was just lucky before. Now I am washed up. My best days are behind me. God isn't blessing me now the way He was back then. The fat lady has sung her song.

Those who live in the past are never there for a good or wise reason. When we say "the old days were better than these," it is a slap in the face of a God who says, "Do not remember the former things, nor consider the things of old. Behold, I will do a new thing, now it shall spring forth; shall you not know it?" (Isaiah 43:18–19). Notice the order. Obeying God's command to turn away from the rearview mirror is essential to positioning yourself to see a "a new thing." Getting hung up on Memory Lane can keep you from recognizing a bright and promising future! As Alexander Graham Bell observed, "When one door closes another opens. But we often look so long and so regretfully upon the closed door that we fail to see the one that has opened for us."

Let me ask you a question. What was your dream back then? Can you remember how God ignited that fire in your belly and put the "oomph" in your soul? If that particular dream cannot be replicated, do you believe the same God who gave it to you then can lead you into another great victory?

Wonderboy

In a well-known baseball movie called *The Natural*, Robert Redford plays the mega-gifted baseball talent named Roy Hobbs. Even in his youth, it becomes abundantly clear to his family and friends that he is going places with his powerful throwing and hitting arm. One night while young Roy is staring out of his bedroom window during a violent thunderstorm, lightning strikes a huge tree and splits it in half. At that very moment Hobbs is struck with an idea—to make a bat out of the felled wood. When he finishes this special project, he carves the name *Wonderboy* into his creation. That bat becomes a powerful symbol of his personal identity, his gift and his dream. With bat in hand, Hobbs firmly believes that he is Wonderboy, the future greatest baseball player ever!

But time and tragedies take their toll. Just as he is about to hit the big time by signing with the Chicago Cubs, he is hurt and hospitalized, and his career seems over.

Sixteen long years later, Hobbs reemerges into the world of baseball hoping to live his dream. He signs on with a "dead from the neck up" team called the New York Knights—his last chance to play for the majors. The first time that he is called to hit a few balls at batting practice, he retrieves Wonderboy from its trusty black case. Wonderboy, the symbol of Hobbs' dreams, inspires him to smack ball after ball into the distant stands while his teammates watch in awe. The Knights go on to win the pennant when Hobbs swats a stunning homerun.

Your success is not dependent on some special time or place, some "never to be captured again" circumstance. The gift is in you.

What is my point? If you keep looking back to the golden years in hopes of finding meaning and reality, you are definitely stuck in the mud on Memory Lane. Things ended well for the hero in this story because he dared to pick up Wonderboy once again. By reaching for that bat he was picking up his dream. He was declaring, "Although my past was brilliant, those weren't the days. I'm reaching for a stunning encore, today, now!" Time had passed and misfortune had befallen him, but Hobbs did not settle into a life of endless gazing into the rearview mirror—nostalgia for what he was in the past.

And what about you? Are you settling for living on Memory Lane? It will bring death long before you die.

Listen carefully: Your success is not dependent on some special time or place, some "never to be captured again" circumstance. The gift is in you (see 1 Peter 4:10). It was not Hobbs' bat that brought him success, it was Hobbs himself. He learned that it was not the object he swung, but the one who swung it that mattered most. The same is true for you! In other words, the same God who was with you back then is still with you right now. Can you trust Him for an exciting encore?

Encore!

God specializes in jaw-dropping encores. Moses could not have experienced anything better than the encore God performed when the Israelites were pressed against the Red Sea with Pharaoh's army in angry pursuit from behind (see Exodus 14:21). What could top the ten plagues that had ravaged Egypt to secure the freedom of a million Israelites? Only Jehovah could send a mighty east wind from heaven and carve out a highway of deliverance through a sea for His people. What an incredible encore!

The famous biblical strong man, Samson, knew all about picking up his vision, his own Wonderboy, again. With great victories for God behind him, the he-man with the she-weakness lost it all by sharing the secret to his great strength with Delilah, who betrayed him and turned him over to the Philistines (see Judges 16). After gouging out his eyes and cutting off his hair, his cruel tormentors attached him to a grinding mill where he spent his days walking in endless circles, a mere shadow of the hero he had once been. Nevertheless, Samson remembered God and prayed in his hour of crisis, "O Sovereign LORD, remember me. O God, please strengthen me just once more, and let me with one blow get revenge on the Philistines for my two eyes" (verse 28, NIV). Positioning himself between the two main pillars of the temple where the Philistines were celebrating, he pushed the entire building down, killing more of God's enemies in his death than he had in his entire life. A powerful encore!

In order to live your life focused through the windshield of faith and hope, you must never succumb to the myth that "the former days were better than these." Whatever your Wonderboy may have been—a successful business enterprise, a fulfilling relationship, a time of great blessing—you still have what it takes to experience a rousing finale! Even if Wonderboy is unrecoverable exactly as it was before, the one who swung it—that's you!—is reading this page. A new day will come as you walk in the fresh vision God gives you, not by staring backward to a time that you can never recapture. Never let the siren song of yesterday rob you of what could be yours right now.

Climb a Tree!

A number of years ago, God blessed my family and me by allowing us to pioneer a brand-new church in the piney woods of East Texas. I mentioned earlier that we were eventually able to purchase four acres of property and build a house right on top of a beautiful, sloping hill. I loved taking our children for walks in the neighboring woods. The sunlight would stab through the tops of the huge swaying trees, blanketing the pine needle-covered ground with its warmth. It was so peaceful. The birds would chirp and sing, while squirrels leaped from treetop to treetop like natural-born acrobats.

There was a rule of thumb for those who liked these kinds of hikes in the forest. If you ever got lost, just climb the tallest tree you could find and you would be able to get your bearings. It was not long before I was glad to have received that bit of country wisdom. One day my two children and I took a long, deep walk in the woods adjoining our land. It was so pleasant and fun that I was not aware of how fast the sun was setting. When it struck me, I also realized that we had walked so far and taken so many turns I was uncertain as to which way would head us back home. Trying to keep my composure in front of the children, I breathed a prayer: *God, You are going to have to help me. Darkness is coming fast. I need direction now.*

Right about then my eyes fell on a tall, old multilimbed oak tree just a few yards away. "I think I am going to climb that tree!" I announced to the children with a smile. Inside I was hoping it was the height that I would need. Climbing from one limb to the next, I finally reached a level just high enough for me to see beyond the forest. There in the distance I spotted the roof of our house. Not long after, we arrived home safe and sound. Climbing a tree had saved us.

A lack of vision for the future is almost always a signal that we need to "climb the tree" of prayer and then ascend to the mountain of the Lord for guidance. The God of the

Bible, our God, is overwhelmingly a God of purpose. He freely gives vision to His children. (We will cover this topic in greater depth in Part 2.) I have never seen retirement mentioned in the Bible, nor have I read that God's people have no hope for a better and brighter future. I have found that God's people are supposed to move forward in faith (see Romans 1:17) and glory.

God does not retire us; He transitions us. As His children, our lives are always scaling upward, moving from challenge to challenge, victory to victory, adventure to adventure and faith to faith.

> But the path of the [uncompromisingly] just and righteous is like the light of dawn, that shines more and more (brighter and clearer) until [it reaches its full strength and glory in] the perfect day [to be prepared].
>
> Proverbs 4:18, AMP

Memories of past successes that magnify the feeling you could never do them again, and that perhaps you should quit, are never true. Second Corinthians 3:18 reminds us: "But we all, with unveiled face, beholding as in a mirror the glory of the Lord, are being transformed into the same image from glory to glory, just as by the Spirit of the Lord."

Time spent with God in prayer carries us above the mundane and into the light of hope. It is in the place of prayer that just one word from the Master can lift us out of the doldrums of depression and into the land of possibility. Time spent in the heights with God allows us to see the "rooftop" of our next destination.

Under the "Son"

When King Solomon was wallowing in confusion and despair as a result of having allowed his foreign, pagan wives to lure him into the darkness of idolatry, he wrote the book of Ecclesiastes. While there are many wonderful truths in this little book, there is an almost melancholy, oft-repeated idea that runs throughout: "What profit has a man from all his labor in which he toils under the sun?" (1:3). "There is nothing new under the sun" (1:9). "I have seen all the works that are done under the sun; and indeed, all is vanity and grasping for the wind" (1:14). I think you get the idea. Anytime Solomon used the words *under the sun*, he was couching despair, anger and disillusionment. That is because the phrase *under the sun* can be easily translated as life without God. At the time he wrote Ecclesiastes, Solomon had lost much of his relationship with the Most High and was reduced to under-the-sun thinking.

This type of thinking is deadly because it causes you to view life only through the lens of your own limited ability. Paul instructed that even on our best day we see only "puzzling reflections in a mirror" (1 Corinthians 13:12, NEB). It is only as we climb the lofty heights into the throne room of God through the shed blood of Christ that a whole new vista of possibilities stretches out before us. I call this "under the Son" thinking. When we live according to under-the-Son thinking we discover that God is not at all finished with us; He always has a "next step" for us to take. This new step may not be a replication of what we experienced in the past, but we are not to be concerned about that. Instead, we must know that success is not measured by wealth, physical prowess or fame.

True success is found in discovering the will of God and doing it.

In 2 Kings 6 we find the prophet Elisha sabotaging the king of Syria's attempts to attack Israel. Each time the Syrian king hatched a plan, God told Elisha exactly what was about to happen. Elisha, in turn, told the king of Israel, who then thwarted the scheme. Finally, a servant of the Syrian king told him that Elisha was the secret informer. The Syrians quickly located Elisha in Dothan and they sprang into action, surrounding the city after nightfall. Second Kings 6:15 tells us that when Elisha's servant arose the next morning and saw the massive army, he panicked and cried, "Alas, my master! What shall we do?"

The servant had an under-the-sun view of the situation. He had no concept of what lay just beyond the natural eye in the realm of the supernatural. One can almost picture Elisha stretching, yawning and looking at his companion with a level of exasperation. He then replied to him with the famous words, "Do not fear, for those who are with us are more than those who are with them" (verse 16). Then Elisha prayed, "LORD, I pray, open his eyes that he may see." When the Lord responded and opened the servant's eyes he saw that "the mountain was full of horses and chariots of fire all around Elisha" (verse 17). What a difference an under-the-Son perspective can make!

Any time that I have felt lost in terms of not knowing where to turn or what my next step should be, I have "climbed the tree" of prayer and meditation in God's Word. This process has never failed to bring fresh direction, allowing me to see above the forest of confusion and frustration to my next destination. Do not let past successes intimidate you into believing nothing great can happen again. Stay under the Son and you will be able to take your next step in God.

Give Me This Mountain!

In the days when the children of Israel crossed over the Jordan and entered into the Promised Land, no two men on earth could claim the achievements of Joshua and Caleb. As Moses' successors they had survived a journey through the wilderness in which one million of their kinsmen had died. They alone had returned from spying out the Promised

If anyone could have "kicked back" with a bowl of giant grapes, a jar of Promised Land honey and a glass of cold Promised Land milk, it was Caleb.

Land with eyes of faith, instead of a paralyzing under-the-sun perspective that proved to be a death sentence for the rest of the wilderness wanderers. God said of Caleb, "But My servant Caleb, because he has a *different spirit* in him and has followed Me fully, I will bring into the land where he went" (Numbers 14:24, emphasis added). Along with Joshua, Caleb had watched the waters of the Jordan divide miraculously. He was one of only two—out of a million people—to successfully eat the fruit of the land! Success was Caleb's middle name. Behind him lay victory after stunning victory.

But Caleb did not stop there. He did not let past successes hinder future exploits. If anyone could have "kicked back" with a bowl of giant grapes, a jar of Promised Land honey and a glass of cold Promised Land milk, it was Caleb. He could have gathered his grandkids around him and talked about the "good old days" when God followed them with the cloud by day and the fire by night. He could have turned their eyes into wide-eyed marbles by talking about the howling east wind that had pushed apart the Red Sea, and how the sea returned to drown Pharaoh's army after the Israelites were safely on the other side. He could have waxed eloquent about the daily manna, water gushing from the rock, Moses' face glowing in the dark and the ten plagues that God had sent to free them from Egypt. Yes, Caleb could have retired, thinking to himself, *There can't be any more to life than what has already taken place!*

I am glad to say that is not what Caleb did. When he was forty years old, he had gone with Joshua and ten others to spy out the Promised Land. God had promised them, "Every place that the sole of your foot will tread upon I have given you" (Joshua 1:3). Caleb took that promise seriously. As they walked throughout their future homeland, they came upon the city of Hebron. It was here that the twelve spies encountered the giants of Anak who struck such fear in their hearts. This place, more than any other, seemed to be invincible. Caleb, however, began to walk on that land, laying claim to where his feet trod. At that moment, Hebron became his God-given dream.

Caleb was destined to pass through 38 more years in the wilderness, enduring all the plagues of the desert, and seven additional years in Canaan experiencing the perils of war before he would gather a group of witnesses with which to approach Joshua. He recounted to his old friend how God had kept him alive for 45 years. He declared that he was yet strong and vital. Then he asked the biggie: "Now therefore, give me this mountain of which the LORD spoke in that day" (Joshua 14:12). The Anakim giants were still there! With this bold declaration, Caleb was staring war straight in the face again—but that did not shake his resolve. Through 45 long years of endurance and war, Caleb had never allowed his dream to die. God honored Caleb and granted his request. What an encore!

Past successes do not give us the right to be intimidated when we are reaching for the sky again, nor do they allow us to drive along for the remainder of our days on the fumes of yesterday's victories. God's dream for you is lifelong and beyond! Henry Ward Beecher wisely stated: "Every tomorrow has two handles. We can take hold of it with the handle of anxiety or the handle of faith." So grab the handle of faith and take your next victory!

As you move further into your destiny, continue to beware of the deceptions of Satan. He will not cease in his efforts to entice you into the past in a number of sinister ways. The next chain that we will uncover is one that keeps you checked in to a place affectionately known as Heartbreak Hotel. Violin music pervades the atmosphere and the food is rich, but the price of the rooms is far too expensive. What will it cost you to linger too long? What price are you willing to pay in order to listen to the lies of the past? Believe me, it is not worth it.

Points to Ponder

1. Have you had a tendency to assess the rearview mirror and say, "Those were the days"? If so, how often and about what?
2. What is your "Wonderboy"? A business? A relationship? An accomplishment? Do you believe that God can bless you with an encore?

Lost Love's Lure

> I looked for the one my heart loves; I looked for him but did not find him.
>
> Song of Songs 3:1, NIV

> The Spirit of the Lord GOD is upon Me, because the LORD has anointed Me . . . to heal the brokenhearted.
>
> Isaiah 61:1

Few things can hold your eyes glued to the rearview mirror like a broken heart. A broken heart is distinctly different from an inordinate attachment. In the latter case it is mostly a matter of deciding to let go. When we have a broken heart, we desperately want *it* to let go of us! Inordinate attachments often come from misplaced sentimentalism. A broken heart is the result of a shattering occurrence.

Isaiah the prophet predicted that one of the key ministries of the Messiah would be to "bind up the brokenhearted" (Isaiah 61:1, NIV). Strong's *Concordance* tells us that *bro-*

kenhearted comes from a Hebrew word meaning "to burst, break in pieces, crush." The prophet went on to predict that the Messiah would "bind up" the broken heart, which means "to bandage, cover, envelop, or enclose." It is not hard to see that a broken heart is serious enough to require a divine touch!

If you are currently experiencing a broken heart, you could probably describe it as the *pain that just keeps on giving*. When suffering from lost love, a tidal wave of emotions crashes against your soul, sweeping all your hopes away in a rush of pain and confusion. Heartbreak is misery to the hundredth power: You cannot eat, sleep or concentrate. When you are suffering from a broken heart, *nothing matters* but the sense of indefinable loss you feel over the object of your affection. You may be suffering from a broken engagement or a broken marriage. You may be suffering the tragic loss of a child or a parent. It does not really matter what caused your broken heart. A broken heart hurts . . . *big time*.

Months may pass (or even longer) after your loss, but sometimes you still find yourself struggling to put the pain and emptiness behind you. During this difficult time, second-guessing yourself can become an art form as you wonder, *What could I have done differently?*

And all the while two words steadily creep up on you, and you do not want to acknowledge them. Yet, time drags on and harsh reality finally reaches your soul with the truth. *It's over.* (We will explore these two life-changing words much more deeply in chapter 8.) Now, though the dust has settled, you just cannot seem to pull yourself away from the memories and the belief that the lost relationship was the real thing. *It should have been the real thing.*

You are faced with a choice: You can resign yourself to never moving on, never loving again and never again grasping life with fresh gusto, or you can walk through this cycle of grief. Truth be known, *the best way out is through.*

Though Heartbreak Hotel actually reflects a condition of the heart and is not an actual place, it might as well be one.

People with broken relationships are particularly vulnerable to driving down Memory Lane. And the next stop for them? The only place Memory Lane leads—*Heartbreak Hotel.* Though Heartbreak Hotel actually reflects a condition of the heart and is not an actual place, it might as well be one. It comes complete with doors, bars and locks. Its residents are living *in a memory*, dying *for a memory*, and longing to *recapture a memory*. They have forfeited all future possibilities for the long-shot hope of recovering a past that has long since *passed*. Even worse, they wistfully *vow* to stay in that place for as long as it takes! "I'll be waiting for you," they cry, "I'll still be around."

Take a leisurely stroll through the lobby of Heartbreak Hotel and you will not observe much interaction. Why should the guests be open to meeting someone new? Any new candidate is compared unfavorably to "the one" who has gone. The heartbroken *want* to be free, but freedom eludes them as they struggle to mend their shattered hearts. Like Humpty Dumpty, they just cannot seem to put it back together again.

The good news is that Jesus Christ came to check us out of the somber halls of Heartbreak Hotel. Now, I can almost guarantee that you will not *feel* like leaving, but departure is preferable to continual suffering. Just in case you need further incentive, there is that little matter of the price of the rooms. The bill is staggering at Heartbreak Hotel, but it is rarely seen until checkout time.

The heartbroken forfeit tomorrow by letting yesterday steal away with today.

It has always helped me to give an emotional situation some time. Just as mud stirred up in a creek will eventually settle, leaving the water clear, so settled emotions clear our hearts to receive truth. God is so wonderful at helping us see other views of what troubles us. There are some facts about love and life that deserve our attention. Let's consider a few possibilities surrounding your heartbreak that may bring hope.

Two Women and a Baby

Perhaps the most famous decision ever made by wise King Solomon took place during a visit from two women and a baby (see 1 Kings 3:16–28). The Bible tells us that the two women were harlots who lived in the same house. Both had borne children within days of each other. One night one of them had rolled over in her sleep and accidentally suffocated her child. Solomon was told by one of the women that the offending mother awakened, saw what had happened and swapped children while the other slept. As Solomon listened, the woman being accused suddenly cried out, "No! But the living one is my son." The first woman quickly protested, "No! But the dead one is your son, and the living one is my son" (verse 22).

True to his reputation, Solomon made a wise decision. "Bring me a sword," he commanded (verse 24). When the sword was in clear view, he said, "Divide the living child in two, and give half to one, and half to the other" (verse 25). What followed is a vivid illustration of what often happens in relationships.

The truth rose quickly to the top. The woman whose son was living cried out, "O my lord, give her the living child, and by no means kill him!" (verse 26). She was willing to release her only son in order to save his life. She was even willing to allow the lying woman to have him, if only he could be spared. She could never have stood by and watched as her child was cut in half. The real mother could not hide her genuine love. The impostor could not conceal her lack of it.

The second woman replied callously, "Let him be neither mine nor yours, but divide him" (verse 26). She cared nothing for the child. Jealousy and envy (masked in lies) were the true motivations of her heart.

Solomon knew it would take a crisis to reveal the truth. One woman cared deeply, the other not at all, which led to a *major revelation*.

Whenever I have heard this story told, the focus has always been on the two women and their opposite reactions. Let's pause a moment and look at it from another angle—the angle of the baby, because sometimes *we are the baby*. We need desperately to see the hearts of those who surround us. It happens like this: A "sword" strikes. It may be a lost relationship, a personal failure or perhaps a business, health or family crisis. In moments like these we are vulnerable and helpless. God, because He is just and loves us deeply, will use these difficult circumstances to show us the hearts of those around us. Do you recall how clearly Jesus saw the heart of Judas? He knew exactly what His inner Twelve were made of, and He knows the same about us and those surrounding us.

In John 15, Jesus promised to prune away any branches that fail to bear fruit in the lives of His children. I believe a huge part of the pruning comes in the area of relationships. Our Lord said by way of illustration that we are the branches, He is the vine and the Father is the vinedresser. As such, He regularly inspects the "branches" of our lives. These "branches" cover a wide spectrum of issues, relationships being a primary area. If a relationship is not bearing fruit the vinedresser moves in with pruning shears in hand. "Every branch in Me that does not bear fruit He takes away" (John 15:2). Did you catch the words *takes away*? Please understand that I am *not* speaking of marriage. First Corinthians 7 makes it clear that within the framework of marriage, we are called upon to bear much dysfunction for the sake of the Lord and the covenant we made in His presence.

Please understand as well that I am not blaming God for your heartbreak! What I *am* saying is that everything He does is *good* and is *for* our good. In your heart of hearts, do you at least sense the possibility that the merciful hand of a loving heavenly Father was involved in the ending of your relationship? I honestly expect for you to respond, "No, Jeff! I'm shattered! God would not do that to me!" Oh, friend, *yes, He would.* Listen to the prophet Hosea: "For He has torn . . . but He will bind us up" (Hosea 6:1). Do you hear that? *He* tears, and *He* binds back up! Here is the truth: *God will prune you now to save you later* and if His pruning brings pain (as it often does) He will also bring the healing.

Think about this: The truth about these two women would *never* have been revealed without Solomon's sword. On the surface the truth was hidden. I am quite sure that the impostor held the child with care. She most likely coddled him, spoke sweet nothings into his ear, tickled him and showed him off to her friends. Nevertheless, I am certain that one day the baby grew up and thanked God for the sword of Solomon! If it were not for the sword, he might have never grown up with his real mother.

Speaking of Himself, Jesus said, "A greater than Solomon is here" (Matthew 12:42). Our "Solomon" is sometimes forced to produce a sword that reveals difficult truth. The saying is true that love is blind. It is also deaf, dumb and stupid. What we *cannot* or *will not* see, God is obliged to show us. We can make bad, emotion-driven decisions that, if not for the mercies of God, could bring even greater damage to us down the road. It may crush you to the ground when a necessary pruning takes place and someone whose heart you thought was with you proves to be otherwise. In the long haul, you will see that it was for your good.

Let me be crystal clear. I am *not* suggesting that all love relationships gone sour were not genuine and required the pruning shears of God. I am only pointing out possibilities to consider. Remember, time is a great revealer. If the shoe we just discussed does not fit your situation, then do not wear it. If it does, then take comfort in knowing that God's protecting hand was involved. This will help you to heal more quickly. Most of all, beloved, *learn to trust the sovereignty of God in your relationships.*

A Broken Heart Is a Broken Heart

Broken hearts can occur in many different contexts. In 2 Samuel 3, the story is told of a man named Paltiel, who had taken as his wife Saul's younger daughter, Michal. The only problem was that Saul had already given Michal in marriage to David (see 1 Samuel 18:27). During the long years of conflict between Saul and David, Saul acted out of spite, and possibly political interests, and gave Michal to Paltiel in marriage. The day arrived when David demanded that his wife be restored to him. When he sent messengers to reclaim her, the Bible records Paltiel's pitiful response as they marched her away: "Her husband . . . went with her, weeping behind her all the way to Bahurim" (2 Samuel 3:16, NIV). Paltiel's reaction was so strong that one of David's messengers, Abner, had to turn around and snap, "Go back!" Although Paltiel and Michal's relationship was not within the framework of God's will, his heart was still broken.

When your heart is shattered, remember the good news: No matter what the context was surrounding your heartbreak, *Jesus wants to heal you.* As we noted at the beginning of this chapter, He was anointed to "bind up" shattered hearts. So how can you check out of Heartbreak Hotel and move on with a restored and joyful heart? How can Jesus "bind up" your wounds? How can you prevent the enemy from using this chain to bind you to a past relationship? (We will explore these questions, but keep in mind that Part 2 gives more compelling reasons to leave behind *anything* that will hold you to the past.)

Be Careful Where You Take It

A broken heart is a desperate condition that can cause us to take desperate measures in attempts to ease the pain. The writer of Proverbs observed that "by sorrow of the heart the spirit is broken" (Proverbs 15:13). Solomon then begs the question in Proverbs 18:14: "But who can bear a broken spirit?" A sorrowful heart breaks the spirit and a broken spirit is *unbearable*!

Due to the "unbearable" pain of a broken heart, we might be tempted to take it for healing where it does not need to go. Allow me to start by listing a few options that definitely will not help.

- *It is futile to try to numb a broken heart by self-medication.* We can self-medicate a shattered heart by abusing substances such as drugs or alcohol. Misusing prescription drugs has also become popular in our day. Numbing a broken heart through self-medication is like throwing gasoline on a fire. It only prolongs the agony. The heart always wakes up again, roaring louder than ever.
- *Denial does not solve a thing.* You cannot deny a broken heart any more than you can deny a broken arm. You may try to push the pain under the surface but, like a jack-in-the-box, it will pop up again. In fact, in a moment we are going to see that one of the crucial steps to healing is to openly and honestly carry your heart to God.
- *Running to another person, or into a "rebound" relationship, is another tactic bound to fail.* This action is not fair, of course, to your heart or to the "lucky" person you have chosen to distract you from your heartache. The

truth will soon come out that rebounding is exactly what you have done, and this will leave you right where you started—alone with a broken heart.
- *The attempt to distract a shattered heart by a flurry of "busyness" is no help either.* This only places a muzzle on it. Busyness *does not* and *cannot* heal a broken heart. The dull ache within will continue to throb when the lights go out, your head hits the pillow and you are alone with *only you*. Remember Proverbs 18:14: "Who can bear a broken spirit?" You cannot "bear" a broken spirit. It must be healed.

Since these options will fail ultimately, what can you do with your broken heart? Let's recall Isaiah 61:1: "The Spirit of the Lord God is upon Me, because the LORD has anointed Me . . . to heal [bind up] the brokenhearted." Remember that the word *bind* means "to bandage, cover, envelop or enclose." This is a beautiful description of what Jesus does with a shattered, broken heart. He envelops it with His presence, encloses it in His protection, covers and bandages it, just as a doctor would fit a cast to a broken leg.

Yet, here is a word to the wise: While Jesus was sent to heal the brokenhearted, we must cooperate with God in obedience to His Word if we want to experience genuine healing and restoration. The following steps are on the path to healing.

1. *Seek genuine repentance if sin was involved in the relationship. Repent* is one of the most beautiful six-letter words in the English language, because it is the doorway to true restoration. In her book *When Godly People Do Ungodly Things* (Broadman & Holman, 2002), Beth Moore writes:

> If you realize you've never repented of the sin, repent with all your might. He will not reject you nor forsake

you. He's been waiting for you to come to Him for relief. He knows better than you do that a guilty conscience will hamstring you from pressing on to take hold of that for which Christ Jesus took hold of you (Philippians 3:12).

2. *Carry your shattered heart to Him.* God is the *only* safe haven for the brokenhearted. David wrote: "The Lord also will be a refuge for the oppressed, a refuge in times of trouble" (Psalm 9:9). The word *refuge* has its root in a word meaning a cliff, or other lofty or inaccessible place. When we carry our broken hearts to God, He hides us away in the cleft of the rock, safe from attack or further damage. I guarantee you, not one thing you say to the Almighty will fall on unsafe ears. You can *break* before Him. Cry. Wail. Yell . . . and then cry some more. *It's okay!* Get it out in the safety of Father God's arms. "Pour out your heart before Him" (Psalm 62:8).
3. *Saturate your soul with His Word.* David declared: "The law of the Lord is perfect, restoring the [whole] person" (Psalm 19:7, AMP). I cannot emphasize enough how important God's Word is to your heart's healing. Notice that David called it *perfect* in its ability to restore the whole person. What you read, listen to and watch—and with whom you associate—will decide where you are five years from now. Read His Word daily, *especially* when your heart has been shattered, for Proverbs 8:34 promises: "Blessed (happy, fortunate, to be envied) is the man who listens to me, watching *daily* at my gates" (AMP, emphasis added).
4. *Be patient with the healing process.* In the Bible we find two kinds of healings. The first is *instantaneous*, as in the case of the woman with the issue of blood (see Mark 5:25–34). The second is *progressive*, as illustrated by the story of the blind man who required two touches from Christ before seeing clearly (see Mark 8:22–26).

> There will be times when it seems as though the pain in your heart will never end, but give it time. It will. Remember Luke 8:15: "These are [the people] who, hearing the Word, hold it fast . . . and steadily bring forth fruit with patience" (AMP).

Let Your Heartbreak Birth a Samuel

I want to focus a little more in-depth on the second step above, carrying your broken heart to God, with a biblical example to help you with its application.

Hannah had reached the end of her rope. Something had to give. The future mother of the prophet Samuel was married to a man named Elkanah, as was her nemesis, Peninnah, who made life miserable for Hannah. Of the two, Peninnah had borne sons and daughters to Elkanah, while Hannah was barren. Based on this fact, Peninnah "provoked her severely, to make her miserable" (1 Samuel 1:6). It is extremely difficult to be ridiculed endlessly for something you cannot do anything to change—yet this is what Hannah endured.

Being Levites, Elkanah's family made an annual journey to the Tabernacle in Shiloh to worship and to sacrifice to the Lord of hosts. Hannah chose one of these occasions to find a quiet place and pour her heart out to God. "And she was in bitterness of soul, and prayed to the LORD and wept in anguish" (verse 10). In her desperation, Hannah prayed that God would give her a son. She promised that if He answered her prayer, she would dedicate her son to serve God all the days of his life, and that no razor would ever come upon his head.

Watching Hannah from a distance was Eli the priest, who was sitting on the seat by the doorpost of the Tabernacle. Hannah was so heartbroken and grieved that Scripture says "her lips moved, but her voice was not heard" (verse 13). Eli assumed she was drunk and proceeded to rebuke her.

Hannah protested, stating that she was not drunk at all, but instead, "out of the abundance of my complaint and grief I have spoken until now" (verse 16). Once he understood the situation, Eli blessed her by saying, "Go in peace, and the God of Israel grant your petition which you have asked of Him" (verse 17). Soon thereafter she conceived Samuel, an anointed priest and judge of Israel for years to come!

Without question, Hannah had been heartbroken, but she took her shattered heart where it needed to go—she "broke" in the direction of God. Here is a wonderful fact: *God can cause your painful experience to birth a Samuel.* He can and will bring something good out of your pain. Hannah could have become bitter and angry, and as a result, lived a miserable life the rest of her days. Instead, she broke toward God. He took her pain and birthed an incredible blessing, a prophet and a father to the nation named Samuel, who anointed David as king of Israel.

On a personal note, I have never experienced heartbreak that God did not use to birth a Samuel . . . *if I broke toward Him.* I recall vividly that it was on the heels of heartbreak that I first gave my heart to Christ. And it was in the midst of heartbreak that God used me to birth a multi-thousand-member church. After Hannah broke toward God, Scripture says that "the woman went her way and ate, and her face was no longer sad" (verse 18). The burden was lifted, and the issue was settled in heaven's court. Remember, God never wastes our pain.

Reasons and Seasons

We have seen that simply knowing and trusting God's sovereign protection can help to heal a broken heart. Added to this, repentance from sin, carrying our pain to Him, saturating our minds with His Word and exercising patience also expedite the healing process. I would like to mention

Seasonal people play significant roles in our growth as human beings; they leave permanent marks on our souls.

another important area that can help you through any heartbreak. It has been noted that people come into our lives for one of three purposes—some for a *reason,* some for a *season* and some for *life.* This principle is clearly illustrated in Scripture, and I have experienced it many times. As I look back, I can recall people who have entered my life for brief periods. They were usually an answer to a prayer or perhaps even to a cry for help. These people are generally sent more for a *reason* than a relationship, whether it is to bring a much-needed word of direction or a note of encouragement. Once the mission is accomplished they usually move on. You might say that I am a "reason" person to you right now!

At other times, people have entered my life for a *season.* Actually, most relationships fit into the *seasonal* category. This type of relationship typically lasts longer than the "reasonal" one. It can be a friendship, romance, business relationship or the result of mutual interests such as child rearing, a hobby or a spiritual pursuit. Whatever the pull, we "connect" with seasonal people and lower the drawbridge of our hearts to them.

Seasonal people play significant roles in our growth as human beings; they leave permanent marks on our souls. Though we may not be aware of it, their views of life, how they respond to adversity, and their personality strengths and weaknesses all play a part in shaping whom we are to become. Yet, as the seasons of our lives change—we graduate, find a new job, move to another town—our "seasonal" relationships change as well. "To everything there is a season, a time for every purpose under heaven" (Ecclesiastes 3:1).

Finally, there are those special relationships that come for *life. Life-longers* typically include spouses, children and rare friendships from God. Life-longers typically have no personal agenda and no ulterior motive for being there.

They are marked by *unconditional acceptance*. "A friend loves at all times" (Proverbs 17:17). You can make a total fool of yourself and a lifelong companion will say, "Let's go get a cup of coffee." Lifelong relationships weather every storm. They are there to stay, no matter what. Proverbs 18:24 describes life-longers so well: "There is a friend who sticks closer than a brother."

Much heartbreak takes place when we confuse *reasonal* people with *seasonal* people, and seasonal people with *life-longers*. By confusing the purpose of a relationship we open ourselves to hurt. What do you do when a relationship you assumed was forever suddenly ends? How do you cope with all the comings, goings and often-painful good-byes of seasonal people? I have misconstrued these relationships and have been extremely hurt, even heartbroken, when a person's purpose was not what I had assumed.

If you want to avoid a long stay in Heartbreak Hotel, you must learn to lean your whole trust upon God when relationships change. Remember Proverbs 3:5: "Trust in the LORD with all your heart, and lean not on your own understanding." This sounds so simple, but I can now say that I *really trust Him* with the comings and goings of people in my life. Your "own understanding" will prompt you to cling and cleave when you should not do so. Your own understanding will lead you to assume that a "reason" person is going to take part in a lifelong relationship. Job 1:21 says: "The LORD gave, and the LORD has taken away; blessed be the name of the LORD." Realize here that Job said this after having lost all of his children to a natural disaster (see verse 19). Imagine his heartbreak! Yet, Job's response virtually guaranteed an early release from Heartbreak Hotel.

Remember these words of wisdom and learn the art of looking up to God and saying, "Lord, I don't understand, but I believe that You are in charge of my relationships, and will even work good from evil." Let me assure you, though people may have left you, God never will! *Move on*. Do not allow the enemy to beat you down constantly with hopelessness. Shake the dust off your feet and forge ahead. You never know what is waiting just beyond the bend! And remember, if you break toward God, your heart will heal.

Points to Ponder

1. Are you currently heartbroken over a severed relationship? If so, how are you coping with it?
2. Be honest enough to admit whether or not you have checked into Heartbreak Hotel. If so, are you willing to take the steps that are necessary to come out? Would you consider placing a time limit on your stay?
3. Can you name at least one person God sent for a reason, for a season and for life? What did or are you learning from each person? Do you see God's hand in the situations?

Failure's Frightening Face

> And Peter remembered the word of Jesus. . . . So he went out and wept bitterly.
>
> Matthew 26:75

> A failure is a man who has blundered and is not able to cash in on the experience.
>
> Anonymous

Have you failed in a way that takes your breath away? Are you in shock that you could have done what you did? Are you hiding in shame from the judgment in others' eyes? Would you give a million dollars for the power to turn back the hands of time and change your past? Perhaps a business venture fell flatter than an American Idol reject. Or you might be reeling from the shock of a failed marriage. Whatever form your failure has taken, even if it was not earthshaking, it still stings. In fact, for some, failure can be so devastating that they never recover.

Failure can hold your eyes (glued) to the rearview mirror and hinder you from stepping into the future a forgiving God wants to give you!

Before you bury yourself over the choices you have made, allow me to remind you that only one man in all of history was failure free: *Jesus of Nazareth.* If you believe the Bible's account of Him, then you know that He alone occupies the rarified air of sinlessness in human form. The rest of humanity enters the world under Adam's failure, both by inheritance and by deed (see Romans 5:17). The Bible declares that every human being alive has failed: "There is none righteous, no, not one" (Romans 3:10). To err is, indeed, human.

Or, to quote a cliché: *Failure is not final or fatal unless you quit.* Failure does knock you off your feet, though, and it will send you reeling down the slippery slope of depression and despair if you allow that to happen. No doubt, failure can set you back and bring significant loss. Worst of all, failure can hold your eyes (glued) to the rearview mirror and hinder you from stepping into the future a forgiving God wants to give you!

So you failed. Okay, you might as well go ahead and say it. Cry, wail, punch a pillow, scream at the top of your lungs, eat a few gallons of chocolate ice cream, throw your pity party and get it over with. The fact that failure happened is no longer the most important issue. Listen closely: You cannot change the facts. It happened. You may be able to buffer some of the aftershock, but think of it this way: If you fell and skinned your knee, you could not "un-skin" it. The top question facing you now is what you will do with the failure, what your response will be.

As I write this book, I am emerging on the other side of several failures in my own life. On the heels of long-term stress with not nearly enough breaks, coupled with some offenses I did not handle properly, I made a series of bad decisions. As a result, the losses have been immense. There have been times I did not think I would ever be able to stand up again and move on. I wish my testimony were different—you have no idea how badly—but, alas, it is not. Trust me, I would shave a few years off of my life if it could empower me to go back and change my mistakes.

In the aftermath of my fresh introduction to the harsh realities of failure, I have had to learn some valuable lessons in order to survive. In this chapter, allow me to share some major lessons from the crucible of my experience.

Don't Underestimate the Enemy

The first is that I have realized in a whole new way that the archenemy of our souls plays major hardball. As Christians we are in a ferocious battle, and the stakes have never been higher. The evil one is not out to make you curse, give you a flat tire or make something go "bump" in the night. He does not walk about in a red suit, brandishing horns and a pitchfork. He is a cold-blooded, ruthless, utterly heartless killer who longs to see God's children live in abject misery and face ultimate destruction.

Jesus gave us the most dead-on description of the devil: "The thief comes only in order to steal and kill and destroy" (John 10:10, AMP). Notice the word *only*, and remember this: The *only* reason Satan ever shows up is to steal, kill or destroy something or someone.

What has infuriated me most is how our enemy lures us into his traps with promises of fulfillment, only to turn and torment us with relentless condemnation once we succumb. Among all of his motives for doing this, his darkest scheme is to sabotage our destinies by chaining us to a past of regrets. "Look at what you've done!" he booms when you resolve to move forward in God's will. "You had it all and squandered it on your stupid mistakes!" he bellows when you attempt to regain lost ground. Condemnation is his bait, accusations are his hook and total defeat is his ultimate intent. If you allow it, *the enemy will use past failures to rob you of your future.*

Navigating through the thick fog of failure can be tricky. You actually must move past two dangerous obstacles following a failure:

1. The consequences of your actions
2. The inner demons of condemnation and guilt, regret and self-inflicted punishment that invariably follow every failure

It is painfully true that long after consequences have come and gone, we must endure the inner struggle.

Two Kinds of Failure

Another major lesson I have learned is there are two different kinds of failure. The first comes from making an honest mistake. This can take the form, for example, of a miscalculation involving finances or a poor decision, in hindsight, about medical care or a job offer. It can be any one of a number of scenarios in which you meant well and gave it your best shot, only to watch your heartfelt efforts crumble before your eyes. Now you are standing in the ashes of disillusionment (maybe even embarrassment), wondering what in the world you did wrong, or how your calculations could have been so misguided. You felt right about it. You probably even prayed about it. After adding up all the options, you chose to go with it . . . and it just did not work.

This scenario takes an added twist when you realize that your failure was aided and abetted by someone else. A business partner left you high and dry, surveying the remains of what he or she refused to take responsibility for. A spouse walked out the door, unwilling to work on a marriage that

Satan's darkest scheme is to sabotage our destinies by chaining us to a past of regrets.

could have survived. A rebellious child snubbed his or her nose at your best efforts to bring discipline and, instead, chose "the broad way" of destruction (see Matthew 7:13–14). These are just a few of the tough situations you must handle after making an honest mistake.

A good part of the difficulty associated with any failure is determined by how great the resulting loss was. If the loss was substantial (as mine was), the temptation to spiral into despair and defeat can be overwhelming. *Why even try again?* we ask ourselves. *What's the use? I have fallen so hard, no one could ever come back from this!* Hear me: As bad as you may feel about what you have done, this simply is not true.

I have a question for you. Do you think God knows you are going to make mistakes? Of course He does! The Bible says, "I am God, and there is no other; I am God, and there is none like me. I make known the end from the beginning" (Isaiah 46:9–10, NIV). I often make the following statement to my parishioners: "God never says, 'Oops!,' and He never says, 'Well, I'll be . . . !'" God is *never* surprised by *anything*.

Do you think that when you made your costly mistake, God turned to the angel Gabriel and said, "Can you believe he [or she] did that? I am shocked!" He *knew* that you were making a miscalculation when you made it! *Then why did He let me do it?* you might be wondering. Because if He did not allow you to make mistakes, you would never learn anything. I guarantee you one thing: If I am going to go through the pain of failure, then by golly I am going to extract something beneficial out of the experience. *A failure not learned from is a failure that you are doomed to repeat.*

If you put up the white flag, surrender and in essence "die" in your failure, you are making the tragic choice to live a life that is constantly viewed through the rearview mirror. There is only one healthy option. You must take your failure

You must take your failure to God and allow Him to restore your strength, hope and confidence.

to God and allow Him to restore your strength, hope and confidence.

The second kind of failure is the kind that leads to bondage. It may result from moral weakness or you may have been seduced into believing some false doctrine, like that involving a cult. Then again, your failure may have involved an addiction to alcohol or drugs or some other dependency. Whatever it was, this kind of failure affects your conscience on a much deeper level because it involves sin, and sin opens the door to condemnation on a far grander scale than does the honest mistake.

Listen closely to the following verse: "Having faith and a *good conscience*, which some having rejected, concerning the faith have suffered shipwreck" (1 Timothy 1:19, emphasis added). Do you see the incredible power of the conscience? To walk around with a guilty conscience is the same as guiding your spiritual ship into a reef! This is why Paul said: "I try with all my strength to always maintain a clear conscience before God and man" (Acts 24:16, TLB).

A guilty conscience affects *everything* you do. That has to be why the apostle listed a clear conscience among his top spiritual priorities! When you have a guilty conscience, your peace with God is gone. Your desire to tell others about Him is gone. Also gone is your excitement about His future plans for your life . . . as is your joy. A healthy fear of God is replaced with an unnatural dread of Him and His judgment. First John 3:21 says: "My dear people, if we cannot be condemned by our own conscience, we need not be afraid in God's presence" (JB, emphasis added).

A guilty conscience is like a thief who calls you terrible names while systematically removing everything dear to you. Your prayer life, Bible study, fellowship with other Christians and confidence toward God are all craftily stolen away while you hide in a cloud of shame.

A guilty conscience is like a thief who calls you terrible names while systematically removing everything dear to you.

The Tyranny of "If Only!"

Well, we might reason, if our failure involved sin, then confession and repentance should get the bugaboo of guilt off of us, right? Not always! The thief often comes in with even greater subtlety by condemning us *after* we have been forgiven. He accomplishes this by stealing our understanding of what the blood of Jesus has already accomplished. The adversary uses what I call the *if only* argument. Following our genuine repentance from a failure involving sin, he sows that little phrase into our unguarded minds. It goes something like this: "God would have forgiven you, *if only* you had not committed *that* sin, but now you have gone too far." Here is another ploy: "Well, yes, you repented. And God could bless you *if only* you had not *repeatedly* sinned, but now you have crossed the line of God's patience." The list of examples is endless.

Satan's greatest hope is that the believer's understanding of grace will be flawed. Why? If our enemy can keep us in partial darkness about the truth surrounding grace, the door to hell's condemnation and harassment will remain opened. And that means we will always live under the tyranny of *if only* guilt. This is because "works righteousness" (right standing with God achieved by our own actions) suggests that our salvation hinges partially on *performance*. If you buy into that belief, you will *never* feel worthy of blessing because you will *always* fail at achieving perfection.

As I write this section, I have decided to don some old, red-tinted sunglasses. At this moment everything I see is red. All objects are visible, yet all have a red tint. I cannot escape it. When I look at my dog he is tinged with red. The furniture, the yard, the sky and this computer can only be seen through a red lens. At the risk of sounding sacrilegious, that is exactly what God has done concerning His children.

Satan is an expert at stealing our understanding of what the blood of Jesus has accomplished.

Jehovah God wears *Son-glasses*! He sees you through the red shed blood of His only begotten Son.

Let the following verse soak deeply into your spirit: "For our sake He made Christ [virtually] to be sin Who knew no sin, so that in and through Him we might become [endued with, viewed as being in, and examples of] the righteousness of God" (2 Corinthians 5:21, AMP). Did you notice the words *viewed as being in the righteousness of God*? Tell yourself that God views you *only* through the blood of His Son! This is the only way He sees you, and nothing you do can add to it, *period.* This may seem to be basic, but do you know how many blood-bought, redeemed children of God struggle endlessly with "residual condemnation" over what God has already forgiven?

Retracing Our Steps

One day a small band of Old Testament prophets realized that God's blessing on their ministry had resulted in cramped quarters. There was no more room for growth. They approached their esteemed leader, Elisha, with a request that would solve the problem: "'Look, the place where we meet with you is too small for us. Let us go to the Jordan, where each of us can get a pole; and let us build a place there for us to live.' And he said, 'Go'" (2 Kings 6:1–2, NIV).

With their master's blessing they set out for the Jordan to cut down trees to build a larger edifice. Before departing, they made one more request of Elisha: "Won't you please come with your servants?" A man of few words, he replied, "I will" (verse 3, NIV). With that settled, the excited prophets were off to do God's work with God's man of the hour, firmly planted in God's will for their lives. I can just imagine them whistling merrily as they made their way through the forest toward the cold, rushing Jordan River. What an ideal situation; things simply could not be any better than this!

Chop! Chop! Chop! The trees fell as the band of prophetic brothers performed their task with gusto. In the heat of excitement, one of the particularly exuberant men swung hard—*and trouble.* "As one of them was cutting down a tree, the iron axhead fell into the water" (2 Kings 6:5, NIV). This was not a happy turn of events for the unnamed prophet. "'Oh, my lord,' he cried out, 'it was borrowed!'" The prophet Elisha, ever the picture of calm, asked the shaken man a question in the next verse that has often haunted me in a good, productive way: "Where did it fall?" (verse 6, NIV).

This beautiful Old Testament story of Elisha and his school of prophets sparkles with spiritual application. In this passage, Elisha is a type of Christ surrounded by his disciples. By following him they had experienced an abundance of blessing—so much so that they were forced to expand their horizons by starting a building program. While in the middle of God's work, following God's anointed man in God's appointed time, one of them lost his "cutting edge."

The lost axhead is a striking metaphor of our own mental and spiritual "cutting edge." For the sake of keeping our subject matter in the bounds of our current subject (failure), the cutting edge represents keenness of mind and spirit. It is a picture of sharp, clear spiritual discernment resulting in wise decision-making. When the axhead flew off the handle, no one was more surprised than the servant. He had experienced a failure right in the middle of doing God's work! He must have been thinking, *How did I not see it coming loose? How did I miss all of the warning signs? Why didn't I stop long enough to take stock of the condition of the ax? Now, it's lost!*

The four powerful words Elisha posed to the servant are the very words we must ask following any failure involving sin: *Where did it fall?* Ponder the following with me regard-

When you first began missing God, a door was opened that needs to be shut, particularly if your failure involved sin leading to bondage.

ing your failure. There was a point of departure, a place where you took a detour into the situation where you now find yourself. At what point did your reason, soundness, spiritual accuracy and knowledge of the truth fly off the handle? Where was your cutting edge lost? What should you have known that slipped right past you, opening the way for your failure?

The unhappy servant was forced to think back to his last swing of the ax, judging approximately where it had disappeared into the waters of the Jordan. This line of thought is exactly what God led me to do following the series of very wrong decisions I had made. He asked, "Jeff, where did it fall? What were the first steps that took you down that deceptive road? When and how did your thinking first begin to cloud?" There is a point at which you, too, made the first faulty decision, where the steering wheel was turned ever so slightly, resulting in your arrival at a destination far away from God's will. You need to discover exactly where that took place.

Here is why doing this is so important: When you first stepped out of God's will, a door was opened that needs to be shut, particularly if your failure involved sin leading to bondage. As Elisha required the servant to go back to the very spot where the loss first occurred, he was leading him in an act of recovery. Going through this process shuts the door the enemy managed to pry open, and allows you to settle accounts and proceed with liberty into your future. This is one instance when assessing the past is healthy.

Now, please listen carefully, because what Elisha did to retrieve the axhead is exactly what we must do in order to recover from failure and restore our "cutting edge." Once shown the place where the axhead disappeared into the water, the prophet proceeded to cut a stick. Then he threw the stick into the Jordan at the spot where the axhead had disappeared. Miraculously, the iron axhead popped to the surface of the water—the only recorded time in history when iron floated like Styrofoam! With typical nonchalance, Elisha commanded, "Lift it out" (verse 7, NIV). The happy and relieved prophet "reached out his hand and took it."

The pathway to the healing of the cross is being ruthlessly honest with God and with yourself.

The Old Testament is filled with types, shadows and pictures of New Testament truth. Elisha placed a wooden stick at the spot where the cutting edge had been lost. I just cannot help but see the cross of Christ anticipated in that picture. Let me put it this way: When you need the cutting edge of spiritual and mental sharpness restored, *apply the cross to where it was lost.*

The cross of Christ is the one sure place of restoration and recovery. Take your pain, disillusionment, anger, shame, frustration, sense of betrayal and discouragement to the foot of the cross. *The cross was exclusively given by God to deal with failure.* Out of its bloodstained wood flows His healing power for every time we stumble, for each and every failure, and all of the painful consequences we face afterward. Believe me, the *only* reason a person draws near to the old, rugged cross is because he or she has acknowledged total failure and wants to embrace God's life-transforming standards.

In my own pain, I slowly began to realize that if I were ever going to get up and live again, I would have to make the choice to be honest with God and with myself. If I did not apply the forgiveness and healing of the cross, my cutting edge would forever remain lost. The pathway to the healing of the cross is being ruthlessly honest with God and yourself. Remember, God will never say, "Well, I'll be . . . !" He already knows everything, including what you need to say to release healing, *so say it.* Tell Him every thought. Pour out all of your emotions. And, above all, be ruthlessly honest.

Once you have allowed Christ to apply the healing of His cross to your soul, the cutting edge you thought was long gone will reappear, floating miraculously to your soul's surface, just as the heavy axhead came to the water's surface for the prophet Elisha! When this happens for you, remember there is still something you have to do. Elisha said, "Lift it out." God can bring the root issue to the surface, but you have to pick it up for yourself. In other words, *get up again*! Whether your failure was an honest mistake or involved sin leading to bondage, you must refuse to stay down another day. Begin to walk in the healing God has brought to your soul. Start reading the Word again. If you have left church, go back! Pray again as you used to. If you need a good reason to pray again, start by praying *for yourself*, because no one needs it more than *you*! Read on to see what I mean.

The Hardest Person to Forgive

Take a moment and walk to the nearest mirror. Now look at your reflection. What do you see? You might say, "Well, I could sure use a face-lift!" or "I never have liked my nose!" You might at first glance say, "There goes that hairline again!" These are all common responses, but that is not what I want you to focus on at this moment. Look into the mirror again. You are now gazing at the hardest person in the world to forgive.

When we refuse to forgive *ourselves* it is as great an act of disobedience as refusing to forgive another. Jesus taught some of His hardest lessons on the topic of forgiveness. He said, "If you forgive men their trespasses, your heavenly Father also will forgive you; but if you do not forgive men their trespasses, neither will your Father forgive your trespasses" (Matthew 6:14–15, RSV). Yet, scores of people live out their lives never forgiving themselves for something God has already forgiven. They never let themselves off the hook.

Forgive yourself! Look in the mirror, take a deep breath and say, "Self, I forgive you!" As we will see in Part 2 of this book, nothing is worth holding you in a past of regret, especially in light of what awaits you in the future!

Now let's keep moving forward to another sinister chain used by our enemy. If you have ever been or are currently tied to the past by a trauma, we are going to find in the next chapter that the God of all hope holds the key to your freedom.

Points to Ponder

1. Have you lost the cutting edge? Have you felt that it was forever irretrievable? If so, would you consider taking the hand of Christ and walking with Him to the place where you first took a misstep?
2. You have repented and know that God has forgiven you, yet the feelings of guilt and condemnation have not fully lifted. Is it possible that you need to make a trip to the nearest mirror and have a forgiveness session with yourself? If so, why not do it today, even right now?

Tied to a Trauma

> I am feeble and severely broken; I groan because of the turmoil of my heart.
>
> Psalm 38:8

> God whispers to us in our pleasures, speaks in our conscience, but shouts in our pains.
>
> C. S. Lewis

There are some needles only God can thread. On our life tapestries, the valley is too deep, the mountain is too high, the danger is too great or the sin is too dark for us to do the mending we need. Yet with His skillful hands of mercy, God grasps the thread of grace and somehow weaves us along a path we could never have followed alone. It is called deliverance, the kind you need when you are tied to the past by a life-altering trauma.

Webster's *Dictionary* defines trauma as "a bodily injury or shock; an emotional shock, often having a lasting psychic

..ect." According to the Department of Veteran's Affairs (see www.ncptsd.va.gov/facts/general/fs_effects.html):

> The survivor experiences again the same mental, emotional, and physical experiences that occurred during or just after the trauma. These include thinking about the trauma, seeing images of the event, feeling agitated, and having physical sensations like those that occurred during the trauma.

Experiencing trouble sleeping and concentrating, as well as depression, despair, hopelessness and the loss of important beliefs can also accompany trauma.

Christians are not exempt from trauma. Jesus forewarned that "in the world you will have tribulation; but be of good cheer, I have overcome the world" (John 16:33). According to *Vine's Complete Dictionary of Old and New Testament Words* (Thomas Nelson, 1985), the word *tribulation* comes from the Greek word *thlipsis*, which means "a pressing, pressure, anything which burdens the spirit." Strong's *Concordance* adds "affliction, trouble, anguish, and persecution" to the mix. Putting all of this together we see the distress inherent in tribulation.

Yet, tribulation is a part of our world. There is no escaping it. Jesus predicted that tribulation would only increase as the time of His return neared: "For then shall be great tribulation, such as was not since the beginning of the world to this time, no, nor ever shall be" (Matthew 24:21, KJV). Other Bible versions translate the word *tribulation* as "persecution" (TLB), "great misery" (PHILLIPS), "great distress" (JB) and "terrible trouble" (GNT). *Tribulation* could easily be a synonym for *trauma*.

I certainly will not pretend to know the answer to the age-old question of why God's children suffer. Remember that Jesus was addressing His own people when He stated that they would suffer much tribulation. Volumes have been written on this topic and it still has not been fully answered. There is a mystery as to why good, God-fearing, innocent people suffer. We do have the assurance, however, that whatever we face, He has already promised we would overcome it. As David observed, "Many are the afflictions of the righteous, but the LORD delivers him out of them all" (Psalm 34:19).

What I do want to do here is help shift our sight from an unhealthy focus on the past to the picture of the broad view before us. I will attempt to do this, partially in this chapter and more fully in Part 2. Let's start by exploring a sampling of three traumatic events that many people are all too familiar with.

An Overwhelming Loss

The book of Ruth is a love story that grows out of the great pain a family endures, particularly a woman named Naomi and her daughter-in-law Ruth. The drama begins during the time in Bible history when judges ruled Israel prior to the establishment of kings. Around the time of the well-known judge Gideon, a famine ravaged the land. As a result, Naomi's husband, Elimelech, moved Naomi and their two sons to the country of Moab where they made their home for about ten years.

Once in Moab, Naomi's heartbreaks fell like dominoes. First, "Elimelech, Naomi's husband, died" (Ruth 1:3). Naomi's two sons, Mahlon and Chilion, married two Moabite women, Ruth and Orpah. As time passed both sons also died, leaving her with two daughters-in-law and an aching, bitter heart. To top it off, when Naomi decided to return to her homeland, Orpah stayed behind with "her people and . . . her gods" (verse 15). No wonder Naomi cried out to Ruth and Orpah: "The hand of the LORD has gone out against me!" (verse 13).

The American Journal of Psychiatry states: "The death of a spouse is one of the most stressful life events, and bereavement is a known risk factor for health problems." The article goes on to report:

> A new study shows that the risk of long-term mental and physical problems is even greater among those who suffer "traumatic grief," a psychiatric condition of profound emotional trauma . . . triggered by a spouse's death. (See www.lifepositive.com/stress.html.)

According to statistics, Naomi was hit hard. It should also be noted that in her cultural framework her financial situation could not have been more precarious, due to the death of every male family member. All of these things coupled together spelled *trauma*.

A Needless Accident

It was a gorgeous, sunny Wednesday in the summer of 1985, and Pittsburgh could not have looked more beautiful. Bill had just wrapped up a day's work as a perfusionist (a medical professional who employs artificial blood pumps to propel open-heart surgery patients' blood through their body tissue during surgery) and was on his way home. He and his wife, Marcia, had recently recommitted to their marriage and he was looking forward to spending some time with her. On the way home, he drove by his brother's house and noticed his motorcycle outside the garage. After stopping to chat for a bit, he asked if his brother would mind if he borrowed the motorcycle to make the journey to his in-laws' home where Marcia waited. Feeling a bit of concern over his inexperience, he nevertheless cranked it and was off.

As Bill approached a ramp leading to a bridge, it seemed as if everything suddenly went into slow motion. He negotiated a bend too widely and did not lean into the bike far enough. He knew he was going to wreck. His right shoulder slammed into the first girder on the bridge and in an instant he hit the second girder with the left side of his head. As the motorcycle careened out from under him, end over end, down the bridge, Bill finally landed in the middle of the bridge roadway.

Bill never lost consciousness. At first he could not move at all, but gradually bodily movement returned—except to his right arm. Grim-faced doctors informed him he would never regain use of it. This destroyed his career—and many other hopes and dreams. For fifteen long years, Bill would be tied to the past by trauma, struggling with the dark demon of depression.

A Senseless Tragedy

Charles Haddon Spurgeon was called the "prince of preachers" in nineteenth-century London where, as a young man of only 21, he assumed the pastorate of a small, dying church. His oratorical skills quickly became legendary. The once struggling church rapidly outgrew its building, forcing the burgeoning congregation to seek a much larger facility. Mr. Spurgeon frequently stepped out in faith by renting huge facilities to accommodate the massive crowds that came to hear him. His voice was often described as sounding "like a bell" and could easily be heard by a crowd numbering from five to ten thousand during a time when no audio aids existed!

On one occasion, the popular preacher held a service at London's famous Surrey Music Hall. It seated upwards of ten thousand people and, on this fateful night, according to one report, was filled to overflowing with twelve thousand in attendance. Many thousands more were turned away at the doors. As Mr. Spurgeon stepped to the pulpit to deliver his message, someone in the crowd suddenly cried, "Fire!" Panic ensued. The huge crowd fled the building in terror from a fire that never existed. The stunned preacher stood helpless and watching in horror as several people were trampled to death and scores of others were injured. The following morning the London newspapers were less than kind to the grief-stricken preacher, both criticizing and vilifying him for having such a large crowd in attendance.

Spurgeon was traumatized by the event. In *Lectures to My Students* (Baker, 1997), he wrote of the ordeal:

> To the lot of few does it fall to pass through such a horror of great darkness as that which fell upon me after the deplorable accident at the Surrey Music Hall. I was pressed beyond measure and out of bounds with an enormous weight of misery. The tumult, the panic, the deaths, were day and night before me, and made life a burden.

It took an act of God to deliver the great preacher from this terrible trauma.

An Overview

We have considered an overwhelming loss, a terrible accident and a senseless tragedy. They all led to trauma. Each event chained its victim to the past until God in His mercy set that individual free. *Yet, I do not believe any of these examples quite reaches the level of trauma that the disciples must have experienced leading up to and following the crucifixion of Jesus Christ.* Who among us can begin to imagine what must have gone through their minds as they watched their Lord being beaten beyond recognition and then murdered on the worst instrument of torture known to the ancient world? The Rock they had followed for three years, the one for whom they had forsaken all, was crushed before their eyes in a nightmare of bloodthirsty persecution. On top of that trauma lay the double whammy of guilt. They had all forsaken Him in His greatest hour of need: "Then

The Rock they had followed for three years, the one for whom they had forsaken all, was crushed before their eyes in a nightmare of bloodthirsty persecution.

all the disciples forsook Him and fled" (Matthew 26:56).

The death of Christ also spelled the death of their dream. He had been their hope of a better future. They had been *so positive* that He would usher in a brand-new age of peace and prosperity, far removed from the loathsome Roman tyranny. The disciples who had once stood next to Jesus before huge crowds were now hiding behind locked doors, not knowing what to do now that their leader was gone (see John 20:19–26). Frightened and confused, Peter and a few others even tried returning to the life of fishing they had once known (see John 21:3). It would require several special visitations from Jesus in order to set them free.

A Place Called Emmaus

On the very day Christ was resurrected from the dead, two lone figures walked slowly down a dusty road leading out of Jerusalem (see Luke 24:13–35). One of them was named Cleopas, while the other's name remains unknown. Their minds were still reeling from the events that had recently transpired. They, too, were struggling with the double-edged sword of trauma and guilt. How could Jesus—who had always seemed to be in control both in the good times and in the bad—have come to such a tragic and gruesome end? Their hopes were cruelly dashed on the rocks of disillusionment, their hearts broken: "We were hoping that it was He who was going to redeem Israel" (Luke 24:21). Now they needed rest, contemplation and a place to lick their wounds. They chose Emmaus, a small town about seven miles outside of Jerusalem.

Emmaus places are those places to which we flee when painful circumstances multiply to a level that we do not feel

We do not want to be "on" in Emmaus. We want answers to our pain.

we can handle. To us, Emmaus may be a lakeside cabin or perhaps another town or city where anonymity enables us to hide in a crowd. Emmaus is a place where no one will call our names. We do not want to be "on" in Emmaus. We want answers to our pain. We head to Emmaus when our minds scream "Tilt!" and our hearts cry "Overload!" The flight response takes over. Those headed to their Emmaus understand these words of David: "Oh, that I had wings like a dove! I would fly away and be at rest" (Psalm 55:6).

My guess is that many reading this book are even at this moment hidden away somewhere in Emmaus. If this is true about you, read on carefully. This section is especially for you.

What makes our Emmaus such a challenge is that we are usually caught between a rock and a "heart" place, which is why we are there in the first place. If not for our hearts being heavily invested in whatever it was that shattered us, it would not have been necessary to go. We usually beat a fast track to Emmaus because we believed in something big time, and that something has either crashed and burned or is on the verge of doing so. It could be that, for whatever reason, the thing we were so ferociously committed to has inexplicably turned on us. The cause of the conflict may be a person, a business deal, a ministry situation, a goal or a dream. Whatever the case, the very fact that our hearts and dreams were exquisitely involved empowers the situation to carry us to the edge.

In Emmaus, the "rock" is usually intense emotional pain, while the "heart place" is the pull of our passion. The classic struggle we experience in Emmaus is a tug-of-war between what we love versus the need to protect ourselves; it is the crossroads between passion and pain. Emmaus often emerges as the battleground where our dreams hang in the balance. Do I go with my passion, even at the expense of all this pain, or do I call it a day and walk away? Do I move into my future despite the issues, or do I fade to black and erect a tombstone that reads "Unable to continue. Can't handle the pain"? Thank God for the truth in what David wrote: "When my spirit was overwhelmed within me, then You knew my path" (Psalm 142:3). Even when we do not know which way to go, Jesus always does!

I recently passed through an Emmaus experience of my own. Through a series of events that felt like a waking nightmare, I experienced the pain of betrayal on a level I never thought was possible. People who had been close to me for years, and who I assumed were lifelong friends, proved to be otherwise. I learned the excruciating truth that you never know who is really with you when you are up and strong. Sometimes it takes a vulnerable moment, when your guard is down and you are less than a perfect human being, to see what really lies within those who surround you. Though this situation has begun to work for my good (in the long haul), it was one of the most shattering experiences of my life.

My Emmaus became a little eight-by-ten-foot study into which I withdrew for close to a year. I also retreated into an Emmaus within myself. My exterior surroundings reflected my interior soul. I was emotionally traumatized. Oh, I would come out of my Emmaus by preaching on Sundays or meeting friends for lunch from time to time. Despite the pain, I tried to function to the best of my ability, but I could not deny that something within me had died. If ever I was on the brink of tossing in the towel and walking away from ministry, that was it.

Three ghosts haunted me in my Emmaus place that I will call the three *D*s. Perhaps you have met them, too! They are disillusionment, disappointment and despair:

- What you thought was going to happen did not—*disillusionment.*

- Whom you believed someone to be was proven wrong—*disappointment.*
- The direction you assumed you were going experienced a radical detour—*despair.*

The three *D*s encountered in Emmaus places "rock our world" on a grand scale because of the level of our heart investment. When you really believe something with every fiber of your being—enough to sacrifice your whole heart on its altar—only to see it crumble before you, the stage is set for a major "soul-quake." Hence, Solomon wrote in Proverbs 13:12: "Hope deferred makes the heart *sick*" (emphasis added).

To put it in southern terms, when you are in Emmaus, you are in "a-MAY-ess." (That's "a mess," in case you don't get it.) Emmaus can be an unsettling place because we are forced to ask ourselves hard questions. Let's face it: Something major has happened to something in which we have invested a huge chunk of ourselves. That is not small potatoes. Emmaus forces us to reevaluate some of the things we always assumed were rock solid.

People issues were the source of my "soul-quake" during my Emmaus experience. During this time, I wrestled a great deal with one of Emmaus' chief bandits—cynicism, which is to question the sincerity of people's actions and motives. I never questioned absolute truths like the cleansing blood of Jesus or the trustworthiness of Scripture; but I did reevaluate much of what I had seen being lived out in the Church. It almost ate me alive!

Let me offer a word of encouragement. Though Emmaus experiences and the issues that take us there are painful, in the long run they only work to our good, if we respond correctly. In Emmaus we learn what truly matters to us above all else. When we are shut away in its quiet confines, Emmaus has a way of running our dreams, hopes and aspirations through the sifter of truth, allowing only that which is from God to remain. Emmaus is the place where our compasses are reset, pointing us with renewed intent toward the purposes of God. If we respond wisely, we will emerge from Emmaus with clear, fresh direction. So take heart. If you are in an Emmaus experience right now, hang on; you should soon hear a knock on the door of your heart. Let Him in.

The Solution

Seemingly from nowhere a stranger approached the two dejected travelers headed for Emmaus. It was the resurrected Christ, but Luke records that they did not recognize Him: "Their eyes were restrained, so that they did not know Him" (Luke 24:16). It is encouraging to me that Jesus was keenly aware of the internal struggles the two were experiencing. He came to them in their pain. Remember that knock on your heart's door I just mentioned? Seeming to "play dumb," Jesus asked in verse 17, "What kind of conversation is this that you have with one another as you walk and are sad?"

Needing little encouragement, the two proceeded to pour out their hearts to Him, which leads us to Emmaus rule number one: *You must pour out your heart to God* (as mentioned in chapter 4). King David said: "Trust in Him at all times, you people; *pour out your heart* before Him; God is a refuge for us" (Psalm 62:8, emphasis added). Believe me, nothing you say will shock God. Tell Him about your anger, fear, disillusionment, sin and regrets. Get it all out. As with heartbreak, this is also crucial to your recovery from trauma. He cannot speak to you as He desires until the rubbish clogging your soul is out.

If I may paraphrase their response, it went something like this: "We are deeply troubled about a man named Jesus Christ, a prophet who was mighty in word and deed. The chief priests and our religious leaders arrested Him and handed Him over to the Roman government. A few days ago He was crucified . . . but we were hoping that He would redeem Israel. Now we don't know what to do! His death has traumatized us!" (see Luke 24:19–21).

Notice everything they said about Christ was in the past tense. "He was a prophet. He was crucified. We were hoping. . . ." Tied to the trauma of the crucifixion, their eyes were transfixed on the rearview mirror. Again, I am struck by how important it was to our Lord to restore them. He knew they had to get their hope back if there was any chance for them to reenter the "good fight." This is the key issue in every Emmaus experience.

Though still unrecognized by the two, Scripture records: "Beginning at Moses and all the Prophets, He expounded to them in all the Scriptures *the things concerning Himself*" (verse 27, emphasis added). This brings us to Emmaus rule number two: *We must seek out and receive the Word of the Lord in Emmaus.* Do not while away your time reading popular magazines or escaping into the latest romance novel. This is a life-and-death experience—your future is at stake. Open up your Bible, even if you have to make yourself. God promises that "the law of the Lord is perfect, converting [restoring] the soul" (Psalm 19:7). Like a surgeon's scalpel, the Word of God is uniquely equipped to reach into the delicate corners of our souls and operate on the festering sources of ongoing traumatic pain. Remember, there are some places only God can reach.

As they drew closer to Emmaus, Jesus, like a Master artist, painted a sweeping portrait of Himself on the canvas of their minds. He took their focus off of yesterday's pain and placed it on His ultimate triumph. "Be of good cheer," He had taught them before His death, "I have overcome the world" (John 16:33). They were soon swept away in the blazing truth of all that the Scriptures had predicted concerning His death, burial and resurrection. Their faith was re-ignited by understanding that what they had witnessed was necessary for the redemption of mankind! Jesus, knowing their trauma, ministered to their pain by explaining the depth of God's sovereignty, the height of divine purpose and the width of divine grace. The crucifixion had been God working "*all things* according to the counsel of His will" (Ephesians 1:11, emphasis added).

He took their focus off of yesterday's pain and placed it on His ultimate triumph.

When they arrived at Emmaus, the two disciples made a wise move. This stranger acted as though He would go further down the road, but they requested, "Abide with us" (Luke 24:29). Here we encounter rule number three: *When in Emmaus, never keep Jesus out.* He is your answer, not your problem. Going to Emmaus without inviting Jesus along is to guarantee an unfruitful rehashing of painful events without ever arriving at a healthy solution. You can allow your Emmaus experience to send you spiraling even further down the road of depression and despair, or you can invite Jesus into your pain. The way you respond to Jesus *in* Emmaus will decide how you emerge *from* Emmaus. You need Him there. It was because the two disciples remained open to His input that they experienced restoration.

A Different Kind of Heartburn

Upon arriving, the three travelers sat down to eat. The stranger took bread, blessed and broke it, then gave it to them. At that instant "their eyes were opened and they knew Him; and He vanished from their sight" (Luke 24:31). Mission accomplished! There was no need for the Master to tarry any longer. The formerly downcast disciples were restored. Following Christ's departure, they shared something very telling with one another, "Did

You know you have experienced a breakthrough when spiritual desire returns.

not our heart burn within us while He talked with us on the road, and while He opened the Scriptures to us?" (verse 32).

You know your heart is healed when it is free once again to be set ablaze with holy zeal. Scripture declares that God makes His ministers a flame of fire (see Psalm 104:4). When John Wesley, the founder of Methodism, attended a religious meeting in London on May 24, 1738, he listened to a preacher describe the changes that God works in the heart through faith in Christ. He later testified, "I felt my heart strangely warmed."

Trauma is like cold, wet wood on the hearth of your heart. Once the Word of God has penetrated your soul and the trauma is lifted, the fire of zeal that once burned brightly is rekindled. You know you have experienced a breakthrough when spiritual desire returns. The two disciples were delivered from trauma by spending time with Jesus and listening to His Word. What a simple solution! With a world to conquer and a calling to fulfill, the two formerly traumatized disciples emerged from Emmaus ready to fulfill their destinies: "So they rose up that very hour and returned to Jerusalem" (Luke 24:33).

I do not pretend to understand the level of your trauma. Only you know the depths of your pain—but I do know that Jesus is approaching you just as He did those two traumatized disciples. You may not recognize Him. He may approach in someone else's skin. Yet, you will come to know Him by the effect His Word has on your soul! All He asks from us is to spend time with Him and be willing to receive His Word. Won't you allow Jesus to re-ignite your hope and restore your purpose? If you are in Emmaus, will you pray to Him earnestly, "Abide with me"?

Points to Ponder

1. Are you currently traumatized? If so, are you willing to take the necessary steps to come out?
2. In your trauma have you retreated to an "Emmaus" of your own? If so, have you invited Jesus into your pain?
3. Looking back, are you better or worse off than when your trauma began? Are you growing bitter or better?

Bitten by Bitterness

> Watch out that no bitterness takes root among you.
>
> Hebrews 12:15, TLB

> But hushed be every thought that springs
> From out the bitterness of things.
>
> William Wordsworth

Tradition has it that under Roman law the corpse of a murder victim was tied to its murderer, allowing the spreading decay to slowly infect and execute the killer. This paints a vivid picture of what bitterness can do. By refusing to forgive we can become tied to an offense toward another, and eventually be overcome by the decay. Figuratively speaking, we "carry" the object of our bitterness around with us everywhere we go until it proves the death of us.

- Joan was deeply hurt in a former relationship. Not only did her first husband berate her verbally, but he also beat her so badly one day in a drunken rage that she needed surgery to repair the damage to her body. It is an understatement to say that this abuse was enough to make anyone bitter—anyone who let it, and Joan let it. Everyone who came into her presence heard the same story over and over. To be fair, for a season of time it is therapeutic to "talk out" difficult experiences, not just with God but also with others who can help. When the season goes on for ten years, however, as it has with Joan, this signals a problem with bitterness.

- Tom had tremendous potential in sports. He loved football and was *good* at it. A born quarterback, he was spotted early on by talent scouts, and soon they were making offers. In the meantime, Tom married Susan, who was dead set against the travel and lifestyle that accompany a pro football career. She wanted a husband who was home every day after work, spending time with her and the children. The tension over the issue increased until Tom finally agreed to honor his wife's wishes by bowing out of football and going into business. Eventually they divorced anyway, but by then it was too late for Tom's sports aspirations to materialize. Is he bitter now? Oh, yes! Though he has remarried and twenty years have passed, it is nearly impossible to be around him for five minutes without a trip around the go-nowhere cul-de-sac where Tom's house on Memory Lane is built. He is bitter at Susan, bitter at himself, bitter at the sports world and most of all, bitter at God for letting it all happen.

Bitterness extinguishes the flame of joy and plunges hearts into darkness. It also has an amazing ability to freeze its victims' eyes on the rearview mirror. Life never moves past the moment of time in which they were deeply wounded; they are unable to shake free of past anger and hurt. If they do not forgive, they will spend the rest of their lives stalled on Memory Lane, failing to realize that Memory Lane leads nowhere. It simply goes round and round the same scene in maddening, counterproductive circles. This view from the rearview mirror is one that is old yet amazingly fresh: *old* because the bitter person can carry his or her burden around for decades; *fresh* because bitterness keeps a memory as alive as if it had happened yesterday!

Watch Out!

When I read the words "watch out" in Hebrews 12:15, quoted above, I am reminded of the piney woods of East Texas and the frequent warnings I gave others to be careful when they walked outside. It was a wild, virgin land replete with huge trees, and a gurgling, spring-fed creek wound through. I learned quickly, however, that where there is water there is life, and life there included snakes. Poisonous snakes abounded, particularly in the spring and summer, and the bite of a copperhead or a water moccasin can be deadly.

In similar fashion, the writer of Hebrews cries "watch out" when speaking of the viper of bitterness. Watch where you step, because bitterness is very "snake-like"! You do not often spot a snake until it is too late. In real life snakes hide under rocks or in tall grass or are otherwise well camouflaged. Nobody says, "Well, there's a poisonous snake. I think I'll let it bite me!" No, a person usually steps on it by mistake and painful consequences follow.

Like venom in the physical bloodstream, bitterness injects poison into the spiritual bloodstream. But unlike venom, this spiritual poison not only hurts us—a topic we will address further in a moment—it also hurts others. Speaking of this very thing, the Phillips Modern English version renders Hebrews 12:15 this way: "There can . . . spring up in him a bitter spirit which . . . can . . . *poison the lives of many others*"

The seed of bitterness is sown into the heart by a hurt.

(emphasis added). Not only does bitterness poison the embittered person, but *poisoned* people in turn *poison* others. We cannot harbor a bitter spirit without infecting those around us. A permanent scowl, bitter words, a cynical attitude and violent temper strike at those nearest us, making life miserable for all.

This bitterness that poisons us and others lurks behind what Scripture calls an *offense* or what we might simply refer to as a hurt. According to Strong's *Concordance*, the word *offense* is translated from the Greek root word *skandalon*, from which we get our English word *scandal*. (I wrote about this subject extensively in my last book, *Making It Right When You Feel Wronged*, Chosen Books, 2004.) According to Vine's *Dictionary*, *skandalon* was originally used to describe "the name of the part of a trap to which the bait is attached, hence, the trap or snare itself."

If, for instance, we were speaking of a mousetrap, the "skandalon" of the trap would be the little metal mechanism on which the cheese is placed. When touched it serves as the trigger that springs the trap. In the same way, an offense brought on by hurt is the trigger that springs the trap—the death-dealing blow—of bitterness upon us.

I got a further image of the way an offense can spring out of nowhere one day when I was leaving a conference, walking with another pastor toward my car. Suddenly, just in front of us, a well-dressed woman walking alongside her husband lost her balance. Arms and legs flailing, she lunged forward, crashing to the pavement. There was nothing pretty or graceful about it. She had been tripped by an unnoticed crack in the parking lot surfacing and the rest was history. Bleeding from her knees and greatly embarrassed, she stood back up with our assistance and limped to her car.

Offenses come unexpectedly and blindside us, catching the unwary off guard and making them "trip" in their walk with God.

As my friend and I walked on, the thought occurred to me that what had just happened was a perfect picture of what happens with an offense. *We do not see the hurt coming*. A misspoken word, unfair treatment, a judgmental stare, an intentional slight, rejection, abandonment, abuse—any of a number of possibilities can trip us when we least expect them. The hurt of offense goes deep as we wonder, *How could that person do that? Say that? Insinuate that?* Hurts leave us wounded. Wounds turn to anger. Anger leads to resentment. If left untended the growing resentment will send its deadly roots deep into the soil of our souls.

How dangerous is an offense? Vine's *Dictionary* further defines *offense* as "anything that arouses prejudice, or becomes a hindrance to others, or causes them to fall by the way." An offense has the power to cause the offended to trip and fall in his or her spiritual walk. If not handled properly it can lead to estrangement from God and can ultimately drive the offended person into sin and ruin.

No wonder the writer of Hebrews cried, "Watch out!" The viper of bitterness is underfoot.

There is one good thing about bitterness—its ability to last depends on a *decision*, not on circumstances beyond our control. The only thing that hinders relief for a bitter person is unforgiveness. *The moment you forgive, relief begins!* Jesus taught us, "Your heavenly Father will forgive you if you forgive those who sin against you" (Matthew 6:14, TLB).

The question is this: *How long are you willing to let bitterness hold you chained to the past?* Consider this: The person or people with whom you are bitter are controlling your life until you forgive them. Are they worth that? Do you want to give the very ones you are bitter against that level of power? Again, Jesus said, "If you do not forgive men their sins, your Father will not forgive your sins" (Matthew 6:15, NIV). Until you forgive and release them, your offenders are keeping you from fellowshipping with God, which affects *everything* in your life!

For me this is one of the most somber realities of bitterness. It is natural for the flesh to want to hold a grudge and seek vengeance on those who hurt us. In fact, when you think about it, these are the values our culture glorifies. There are few people in America, for instance, who cannot quote the steely words of Clint Eastwood's "Dirty Harry" character: *Go ahead. Make my day.* He was saying, "Go ahead. Make your move—so I can wreak vengeance on your sorry hide." We love to quote that phrase, but unfortunately a self-destructive philosophy lurks behind it.

I once heard it said that *forgiveness is giving up my right to hate someone for hurting me*. You might reply, "Yes, but it is so hard to do. That person hurt me . . . badly. No one who did what that person did deserves forgiveness!" No, they probably don't. But remember that *you and I* did not deserve God's forgiveness, either. Yet, He forgave us through Christ. Extending forgiveness can be extremely difficult—there is no argument from this corner of the ring—but the consequences of bitterness get tougher in the long haul. Allow me to itemize a few of the guaranteed consequences of bitterness.

- *Bitterness affects your countenance and bearing in a way that Maybelline or Calvin Klein cannot fix.* When Ruth's mother-in-law, Naomi (discussed in the last chapter), returned to her hometown of Bethlehem following ten years in Moab, the women of the town exclaimed, "Is this Naomi?" *Naomi* means "pleasant, delightful, lovely." Notice the way Naomi responded: "Do not call me Naomi; call me Mara [meaning bitter], for the Almighty has dealt very bitterly with me" (Ruth 1:19–20). The book goes on, of course, to show God's amazing providence at work to restore both Ruth and Naomi, but in the beginning Naomi's bitterness had apparently made her difficult to recognize! A furrowed brow, deep lines in the face and hard, angry eyes are a few of the "gifts" delivered by bitterness.

- *Bitterness robs you of your walk with God.* Remember Matthew 6:15: "But if you do not forgive men their sins, your Father will not forgive your sins" (NIV).
- *Bitterness opens the door for satanic attack.* Paul wrote this to the church at Corinth: "If you forgive anyone, I also forgive him. And what I have forgiven—if there was anything to forgive—I have forgiven in the sight of Christ for your sake, in order that Satan might not outwit us. For we are not unaware of his schemes" (2 Corinthians 2:10–11, NIV). In other words, when we fail to forgive we are being "outwitted" by Satan.
- *Bitterness contaminates those closest to you with spiritual defilement.* Hebrews 12:15 reminds us: "See to it . . . that no bitter root grows up to cause trouble and *defile* many" (NIV, emphasis added).
- *Bitterness causes us to miss the grace that God sends our way to help us through personality conflicts.* "See to it that no one misses the grace of God and that no bitter root grows up" (Hebrews 12:15, NIV).
- *Bitterness is detrimental to our health.* Modern medical science seems unanimous in its verdict on the unhealthy effect bitterness has on the physical body, including clotting of the arteries, digestive problems, mental health issues and detriment to our overall well-being.

It is easy to see that bitterness is just plain not worth the time and energy. Once bitterness has grown in the stony soil of an unforgiving heart, it refuses to go away. Bitterness must be removed.

Not one soul among the angry crowd facing Jesus asked for His forgiveness, yet Jesus did not allow the actions of others to control His response.

Whom Are We to Forgive?

Forgiveness can be tricky, because even if we are willing to move forward, it may not be easy to do so. An offending party might not be willing to take part in a reconciliation attempt, for instance. Or the person who induced the hurt might not be available for any number of reasons. In light of this, the following three important examples show those we are to forgive and how we are to go about it in spite of obstacles.

We Are to Forgive Those Who Have Not Asked for Forgiveness

I was once offended by the actions of several people I knew well. Desiring to get it on the table and talk it through, I was met with frustrating indifference toward my attempts to reconcile. What do you do in such a situation, when you have been offended and you need to deal with it? When you are ready to reconcile, and the offending party will not cooperate, much less ask for your forgiveness?

I believe Paul anticipated this scenario when he wrote, "Be at peace with everyone, just as much as possible" (Romans 12:18, TLB). Notice the phrase, *as much as possible*. The apostle anticipated that not everyone would be willing to make things right. Let us also remember our ultimate example, Jesus Christ, who prayed from the cross, "Father, forgive them, for they do not know what they are doing" (Luke 23:34, NIV). Not one soul among the angry crowd facing Jesus asked for His forgiveness, yet Jesus did not allow the actions of others to control His response. He forgave them anyway.

Do not let a bitter root grow, no matter what the offender is or is not doing. If we are going to leave the past behind, we must forgive.

Paul gives us a valuable key in handling someone who has offended us, yet who will not aid us in the process of forgiveness. "When you forgive people for what they have done, I forgive them too. For when I forgive—if, indeed, I need to forgive anything—I do it in Christ's presence because of you" (2 Corinthians 2:10, GNT). Notice the phrase *in Christ's presence*. Paul was stating that though he could not be present when the Corinthian church extended forgiveness in its matters, still he forgave the offenders just as if he were there in person.

Reconciliation takes two, but forgiveness only takes one. Neither the offender nor the one practicing forgiveness—in this case, Paul—had to be together for forgiveness to take place. Let me be careful here. If the offender can be reached, we are commanded by Christ in Matthew 18:15 to go directly to him or her and try to work it out. But if the person or persons will not cooperate in a reconciliation attempt, as in my case, we can still forgive them in Christ's presence! Is it not in the presence of Christ that all forgiveness takes place anyway? Is He not the ultimate witness each time we forgive another? Is He not the one who swings wide our prison door the moment we decide not to let woundedness or anger or bitterness toward those who do not ask for forgiveness chain us to the past?

This is the key that finally set me free. I began to forgive those individuals in the place of prayer "in Christ's presence." After several days of practicing forgiveness between Him and me alone, I began to feel released from the offense.

We Are to Forgive Repeat Offenders

Simon Peter once asked Jesus how many times he was required to forgive an offending brother, perhaps seven times?

The act of forgiveness does not depend on what we consider fair, reasonable or just.

Jesus said, "I tell you, not seven times, but seventy-seven times" (Matthew 18:22, NIV). It is very hard to believe the sincerity of someone who comes to us 77 times asking for forgiveness, but Christ said to do it anyway. This can lead to only one conclusion: The act of forgiveness does not depend on what we consider fair, reasonable or just. We are to forgive no matter how we feel or how something may appear to the natural eye. However, this does not mean we must also reconcile and reenter a relationship. In fact, God may lead you not to reconcile until necessary changes are made, or even not at all. Forgiveness does not require reconciliation, while reconciliation always requires forgiveness.

It comes down to this: *We do not know another person's heart.* That is God's job, and I am very glad of that! How many times have we asked God for forgiveness over a sickeningly repetitive sin in our own lives? Here is an example: Have you ever tried to quit smoking after years of addiction, only to fail over and again? If so, was it not pivotal to your recovery to *know* that even after countless failures He still forgave you? In the same way, Jesus wants us to reflect the nature of our Father in heaven, "for He makes His sun rise on the evil and on the good, and sends rain on the just and on the unjust" (Matthew 5:45).

We Are to Forgive Those Who Are Now Deceased

In speaking of forgiving the deceased, I am not advocating communicating with the dead; I do not believe we can. What I am saying is that we can forgive the deceased who hurt us "in Christ's presence." Our world is filled with people who go through life bleeding over what someone now deceased did to them. These wounded walkers are bitter about it and live chained to a memory. They are literally ruled from the grave by someone who hurt them.

Whether your offender is alive or deceased, the pain, hurt and memories are real. In this case, you can forgive him or her through prayer in the presence of Christ. Whoever that person was does not matter; just go to God in prayer and say something like, "Lord, (name) hurt me. I am offended by what (name) did. I think about this person regularly and what (he or she) did. Lord Jesus, I choose to forgive (name) in Your presence. I release (name) from my anger. I am not You, God. Only You can exercise vengeance. My part is to forgive, which I willingly do in Jesus' name. Amen." As often as you feel the negative emotions rising, pray that prayer. I guarantee you that the power of bitterness will eventually lose its grip.

Just Say It!

The most common statement made to me by those trapped in bitterness is this: "I just do not *feel* like forgiving them. I cannot bring myself to forgive them, because I feel nothing but contempt and hatred." Breaking free from bitterness, for many people, boils down to waiting for the "feeling" to do it. *No feeling, no forgiveness.* News flash! If you feel warmth toward the offender, you are probably not bitter in the first place! The "feeling" is not going to come. I have *never* felt like forgiving someone with whom I was bitter. Forgiveness is a decision, not a feeling.

What are we to do when we do not *feel* like forgiving? The answer is found in that little member that sits between your teeth called *the tongue*. James tells us in chapter 3 of his letter that the tongue is the key to all self-control. "If anyone can control his tongue, it proves that he has perfect control over himself in every other way" (verse 2, TLB). I like the way another Bible version puts it: "For if he can control his tongue he can control every other part of his personality!" (PHILLIPS). This is a stunning truth! I had mistakenly thought that if I just got up early, avoided rich foods and exercised regularly, I was in charge of my life. *No!* Self-control begins and ends with the tongue.

The things we say have far more to do with what direction our lives go than we think. James compares the tongue to a horse's bridle and a ship's rudder. Both are small and inconspicuous in comparison to what they control, yet both are the means by which the direction of the horse and ship is decided. "We can make a large horse turn around and go wherever we want by means of a small bit in his mouth. And a tiny rudder makes a huge ship turn wherever the pilot wants it to go, even though the winds are strong" (verses 3–5, TLB). Catch what James is saying. The direction a large horse or huge ship goes is determined by something small but extremely important. The huge ship is turned around *even though the winds are strong*. Outside circumstances do not decide a ship's direction. The rudder does.

Bitterness is a strong wind. It assails our emotions, hardens our hearts and blows us on a dangerous course, yet the tongue can turn the ship!

James continues with another image: "The tongue is so set among our members that it defiles the whole body, and sets on fire the course of nature" (verse 6). Vine's *Dictionary* defines the word *course* as "the whole round of human activity, as a glowing axle would set on fire the whole wooden wheel." Picture your tongue as the center hub of a wooden wheel, with wooden spokes reaching out to the rim. If the hub were to be set on fire, all the spokes would soon be set ablaze, finally igniting the outer rim. The picture is clear. What we say will affect every touch point of our lives.

When bitterness grips your heart, forgiveness is not a matter of feeling; it is a matter of *doing*—of saying what you should say in the presence of Christ. You have the ability

When bitterness grips your heart, forgiveness is not a matter of feeling; it is a matter of doing—of saying what you should say in the presence of Christ.

to direct your heart, mind, emotions and attitude by the words you choose to say. As mentioned before, I recently needed to forgive some people who had hurt me. It seemed that I just could not find the right feelings. My heart was angry and flirting with bitterness. I found myself talking against them, criticizing them for what they had done. At the same time, however, I was miserable. *Remember this:* The flame of joy is blown out by the cold winds of unforgiveness, eventually plunging our souls into utter darkness. No one is exempt from this.

One morning during my devotional time, I decided just to say it. *"I forgive them,"* I whispered in the presence of Christ. At first it was like pulling a wisdom tooth. *"I forgive them,"* I muttered again, although that time it was a bit easier to say it. With each repetition, declaring my forgiveness became easier still. Peace began to replace the sense of spiritual dryness I had come to know so well. Several days in a row I repeated words of forgiveness in His presence, and the tightness in my spirit loosened. Then I began to notice that the more I practiced forgiveness, the less my offenders loomed so largely in my mind. With each passing day the memories of what they had done and the amount of time they occupied my thoughts *lessened*. By my words, I was finally able to forgive.

The moment we practice forgiveness we discover a fresh ability to focus on the future. The scene out of the rearview mirror is replaced with an expanded view through the windshield of hope and faith. In fact, I cannot wait to begin Part 2 of our journey—because the future is so much brighter than the past that we almost need sunglasses to look at it! We have examined several chains that can cause a backward focus and hold us captive. Now we are going to discover what awaits us on the other side of victory.

Points to Ponder

1. Has an offense begun to put down roots of bitterness in your soul? If so, what will your next step be?
2. Have you encountered resistance or impossibility in your attempts to reconcile with an offender? If so, can you try forgiving him or her in the presence of Christ?
3. Have you discovered that your biggest obstacle in forgiving is your emotions? If so, why not try forgiving the person out loud as much as possible?

Part 2

The View through the Windshield

Do not remember the former things, nor consider the things of old. Behold, I will do a new thing, now it shall spring forth.

Isaiah 43:18–19

Your past is important, but . . . it is not nearly as important to your present as the way you see your future.

Dr. Tony Campolo

Has Anyone Told You It's Over?

> To everything there is a season . . . a time to keep, and a time to throw away.
>
> Ecclesiastes 3:1, 6

> The only way to move into the future is to let go of the past.
>
> Robert Kriegel

The End. How many times have these brief words brought closure to some aspect of our lives? From the time we were children listening to fairytales we learned that life has its beginnings, middles and endings . . . childhood, school, fleeting friendships, Super Bowls . . . many events in our lives have all come to an end. No problem, right? Well, not necessarily. There are times when we discover that *The End* is not easy to accept at all.

What about that relationship you thought would last forever? Is *The End* now etched all over it? What about that "dream job" that seemed custom-designed to skyrocket you to fulfillment and success? Is it unraveling around you? What about the consequences surrounding a terrible miscalculation or mistake you made? Does it now seem impossible to pull everything back to normal? Your eyes linger on the rearview mirror, on the thing that you have held dear, but you know that *The End* is inevitable.

There is something otherworldly about seeing something end that you thought would last forever. As if watching a motion picture, oddly separated from scenes that were once real, you seem unable to grasp the reality that the credits have started to roll. And when *The End* appears on the screen of your mind, you just cannot make it register. *How could he or she be gone? How could I have lost that? What happened? And how? It can't be!* Yet, as the screen goes black, you have to face the truth. *It can be over, and it is.*

At this juncture you face a defining moment—a *major* moment. *The End* can truly spell *the end* of any meaningful existence for you if you let it—and you *can* let it. Many have before you and many more shall after you are gone. But here is the twist: You can allow *The End* to herald *The Opening* of a new curtain on the stage of your future. I have a news flash. No one can make this decision but *you*.

Let me be plain. You can watch endless reruns of if only's, what if's and why me's, or you can suck in a deep breath, pick yourself up and find out what God has for you *right now*. There is one stipulation. You must let go and accept the reality that *it* (whatever "it" happens to be) is *over*. Listen—you can regret something to death. You can pine over a loss until both *you* and *it* are fossilized. There comes a moment of reckoning when a burial must take place—but the tombstone erected overhead must read, "It's over."

It's over has a certain ring to it, don't you think? It bears the sound of finality. You cannot argue with it, because *it's over*. You cannot debate with it, because *it's over*. These two words shut the door, close the lid, say good night and walk into the gray mist of yesterday never to reappear. *What "was" no longer "is."* You must come to terms with *it's over* because . . . it is already gone! *It's over* spells a death, a non-negotiable departure—but once accepted, nothing raises the curtain on the future more wonderfully and breathtakingly than these two concluding words! So, if something is *over* in your life, breathe deeply, turn, walk away and never look back. A brand-new season is awaiting your arrival. As Solomon wrote, "There is . . . a time to keep, and a time to throw away" (Ecclesiastes 3:1, 6).

There comes a time when a burial must take place, and the tombstone erected overhead must read, "It's over."

A Door and a Double Message

Let's pretend you are facing a door. It stands in a dark, rather ominous room of shades and shadows. There is a brief message scrawled across it that reads, "The End." The doorknob is old and worn. You know that you must turn it. *It's time.* After all, what is left but to admit the end has arrived, and then move forward? Tentatively, you twist the knob and, as the door swings open, you are stunned to see a huge, lush forest just beyond. Thousands of stately green trees are bending and bowing before a brisk spring wind. Birds and wildlife are basking happily in a glorious refuge of woods and pine needle carpet. The welcoming sun shines down richly, its bright rays poking through the rich green canopy, bringing warmth and life. Everything about it is fresh and exhilarating. *Is this Utopia?* No, *it is your new beginning.*

Staring transfixed at this beautiful scene, you suddenly hear the door close behind you. Turning to look, you notice a message scrawled on the "new" side as well. It reads, "Endings bring new beginnings." Now you understand. Your new beginning could not begin until your ending had ended!

Your new beginning could not begin until your ending had ended!

We have quoted the words of Isaiah 43:18–19 several times, but let them soak in once again. Keep in mind as you read that Isaiah penned these words well over a century before the events took place! "Do not remember the former things, nor consider the things of old. Behold, I will do a new thing, now it shall spring forth; shall you not know it?" Remember the pattern. You must first *let go* of what is behind you—not blanking it out as though you have some kind of amnesia, but instead willingly releasing it. And then? Behold, a "new thing" emerges, *God's next step*. He has just been waiting for you to let go of what was already gone.

A man aspiring to be Jesus' disciple said to Him, "Sir, when my father is dead, then I will follow you." Jesus' reply to him was, "Follow me *now*! Let those who are spiritually dead care for their own dead" (Matthew 8:21–22, TLB). Jesus was not being callous or insensitive. He recognized that this man's attachment to someone else was hindering his ability to follow the will of God. Just as Lot's wife was inordinately attached to Sodom, this man's father represented all the young man had ever known, and he was hesitant to let go—even to answer the call of the Master. Christ could almost be heard to say, *Let the dead past be buried as it should be.* This is advice for you as well if you are going to walk through the door of your own new beginnings.

Old Things, New Options

In Isaiah's exhortation not to remember the former things, he was telling the children of Israel, who had been languishing in Babylonian captivity for seventy long, grueling years, to take their eyes off of a dead past and walk through the door that led to the new thing God was about to do.

With this exhortation, which rang out like a church bell when the time of its fulfillment came, the eagle-eyed prophet was addressing two separate issues—one positive and the other negative. The negative issue concerned their captivity. Think back for a moment to chapter 6, where we discussed becoming tied to a trauma. *Traumatic* would be the operative word to describe the Babylonian captivity. Another great prophet, the weeping Jeremiah, was an eyewitness to the tragic spectacle of God's chosen people being carried away to Babylon in chains. Racked with grief, he wrote, "My eyes fail with tears, my heart is troubled" (Lamentations 2:11). His description of their pitiful condition is heart wrenching. "Now their appearance is blacker than soot; they go unrecognized in the streets; their skin clings to their bones, it has become as dry as wood" (4:8).

Now seventy years later the Israelites could hear the echo of the former prophet Isaiah boldly commanding the soon-to-be-freed Israelites to let go of the former things and cast a positive eye on the future. In essence, he was telling them, "Take your minds off the pain of your past. Forget the humiliation; it is a new day! Get excited, look forward, something new is about to happen. Tear your minds away from what you lost, what you suffered, what you felt and what you cannot undo." The prophet's message can be summed up in those two words vital for the new life to come: *It's over.*

Letting go of the past was an option they could not afford to refuse. If the Israelites had not let go, they would not have been capable of recognizing the "new thing" God was doing. This cuts to the chase of why I wrote this book. The serpent beguiles us into thinking that the past is worth clinging to, or that failures and mistakes such as those made by Israel render us incapable of breaking the punishing chains that bind us. *This is a lie!* Though there may be a season of chastening, it will not endure for an eternity: "For His

God's new future was sprouting up around them at the very moment they were lingering between a troubled past and the clarion call to step into a brand-new blessing.

anger is but for a moment, His favor is for life; weeping may endure for a night, but joy comes in the morning" (Psalm 30:5). God always extends His hand of mercy and bids us step into a new place with Him.

Part of Isaiah's exhortation about the new thing was this fact: *Now it shall spring forth.* The original Hebrew can be translated more precisely as: "Even now it sprouts up." Isaiah was actually saying, "The first green sprouts of your new beginning are already poking up out of the ground." In other words, *God's new future was sprouting up around them at the very moment they were lingering between a troubled past and the clarion call to step into a brand-new blessing.*

In the verses just prior to Isaiah's exhortation to release the painful past, the words turned Israel's attention to another historic release: "Thus says the LORD, who makes a way in the sea and a path through the mighty waters" (Isaiah 43:16). In this passage he was clearly referring to the stunning parting of the Red Sea. He continued with the assurance that "the army and the power . . . are extinguished" (verse 17). Not only had Israel's ancestors walked across the sea on dry ground, but Pharaoh's army had been dramatically drowned when the waters returned to normal at just the right moment. What was Isaiah's point? *The Israelites were supposed to focus on that magnificent deliverance in order to stir their faith.* His words were calling them to *remember*. This is another case in which assessing the past was redemptive.

Actually, God was about to do something even mightier than before. History shows not only that Israel was delivered from Babylonian oppression, which Isaiah also prophesied would happen, but also that she emerged from Babylon freed of her longtime bondage to idol worship. Do you remember how, during the Babylonian captivity, the Hebrews

Shadrach, Meshach and Abednego were cast into the fiery oven for refusing to bow to a Babylonian idol (see Daniel 3)? And how they emerged miraculously unharmed? Only the ropes that had bound them were burned away. This was a stunning picture of exactly what God was now going to do for the entire nation of Israel. Cast into the fiery oven of Babylonian persecution for seventy years, they were about to emerge unharmed—with the ropes of idolatry that had bound them completely burned away. Add to that the promise in Jeremiah 31:33 that God was going to write His law on their hearts and there was indeed a "new thing" coming around the bend.

Now, I want you to be sure to catch Isaiah's next question. Be careful not to miss its significance. Turning his prophetic gaze to a people on the tail end of a nightmare, and at the beginning of a brand-new horizon, he asked, "Shall you not know it?" (Isaiah 43:19). Once again, the original Hebrew can be translated more starkly. It is rendered, "Will you not give heed to it?" Better still, "Will you then not regard it?" In other words, if they refused to let go of the "former things," they would be paralyzed in their ability to respond to what God was about to do.

Listen to one commentator's take on this verse from *The Pulpit Commentary* (Eerdman's, 1977):

> Events are shaping themselves—the deliverance approaches. Will not the exiled people, whom Isaiah addresses, turn their thoughts this way, and let the idea of deliverance take possession of their minds, instead of brooding on past and present sufferings?

The prophecies have foretold their deliverance from this captivity. God has spoken that Cyrus would be his instrument of deliverance (see Isaiah 45:1). Three key leaders— Nehemiah, Ezra and Zerubbabel—will be stirred in their hearts to return to the ravaged city of Jerusalem and rebuild its walls and Temple. Hence, Isaiah's cry of future happiness: "Even now it sprouts up!" Excitement, mingled with anticipation, was beginning to replace depression and despondency among many of God's people: "Even now it springs up!"

As a nation, Israel was faced with a choice. If the people chose to mull over the past and wring their hands over present circumstances, their ability to respond to what was already sprouting up around them was in jeopardy. They could live in past defeat and failure, allowing it to dictate their future, or they could choose to believe in God's mercy and step into a brand-new day.

Before we look at how Israel responded, let me take a moment to talk straight with you. The bit of Bible history we have just delved into is a vivid illustration of what so many people experience in their lives. Perhaps you are one of them. As mentioned in chapter 5, failure and its resulting consequences can lure us into remaining stuck in the mud of past defeats. We convince ourselves that it is "only right" to indulge in self-inflicted punishment. *After all*, we reason, *we deserve it*. But that is not the way God thinks. Did you know that right now God is preparing a table before you in the very presence of your enemies (see Psalm 23)? In your darkest hour, God is already setting you up for a blessing.

God conducts funerals for failed pasts all the time. He regularly buries the very things we want to set up camp on. "For as the heavens are high above the earth, so great is His mercy toward those who fear Him; as far as the east is from the west, so far has He removed our transgressions from us" (Psalm 103:11–12). The distance between east and west is infinite—and that is how far God removes the guilt of our sins from us. Speaking further through the prophet Isaiah, the Lord spoke: "I, even I, am He who blots out your transgressions for My own sake; and I will not remember your sins" (Isaiah 43:25). Either way, it's a win-win situation.

Let's turn for a moment to a powerful example from the life of King David that shows how to let go and embrace a new day. Then we will return to the choice Israel made.

There are levels of grief that take you so far down not even a spatula can scoop you up.

Two Funerals and a Baby

It was a very somber day in the court of King David. Grief hung like a thick cloud in the air. David's child, born of Bathsheba following their adulterous union, was near death. As the story is told in 2 Samuel 12, the king was doing all he could to prevent the inevitable: "David therefore pleaded with God for the child, and David fasted and went in and lay all night on the ground" (verse 16). These efforts were to no avail, for Nathan the prophet had already spoken: "The child also who is born to you shall surely die" (verse 14). Nevertheless, David did his best to reverse God's judgment.

Surely the demons of guilt and condemnation were having a field day with the remorseful king. It is one thing to reap personal consequences for your sin, but quite another for an innocent child to take the hit! Things were so bad with David that his elders could not even pick him up off the ground (see verse 17). There are levels of grief that take you so far down not even a spatula can scoop you up.

The ordeal went on for seven long, unbearable days. Finally, the child died. Now place yourself in the sandals of David's elders and servants. For seven days their king had neither eaten a crumb nor slept nor peeled himself off the floor. His beard was scraggly, his hair matted, his face long and drawn. Frankly, they were concerned that he might do something stupid.

> And the servants of David were afraid to tell him that the child was dead. For they said, "Indeed, while the child was alive, we

The End scrolled across the screen of his mind. He decided then and there not to allow the tragedy to dictate the terms of his future.

> spoke to him, and he would not heed our voice. How can we tell him that the child is dead? He may do some harm!"
>
> verse 18

The Bible does not say this, but I would not be surprised to learn that the unnerved servants drew straws to decide who would tell him the bad news. Nobody had to tell him, however, because David heard the guarded whispers. "Is the child dead?" he asked.

"He is dead," came the somber reply (see verse 19). Follow David's response carefully, for he actually oversaw two funerals following that announcement: the funeral of his son and the funeral in which he buried a past he could do nothing about.

First he got up. "So David arose from the ground" (verse 20). When something is *over* you are not supposed to stay down; *you arise*. Rising is the first step to dusting yourself off and moving on in the things of God. By rising, David was coming to terms with "it's over" and taking the first step to recovery. Please know, David *did* have other options. He could have ceased living on the spot. He could have given the remainder of his life over to self-inflicted punishment for his mistakes. He could have become a morose, depressed shadow of the man he had once been, but instead, *he got up*.

Allow me to meddle a bit. *Do you need to get up?* Have you been wallowing in the sorrow of something you cannot do anything about? Is it time for you to rise from a bed of sorrow or an attitude or mentality of defeat in order to *move on*?

Next, he removed all the signs of grief. "So David . . . washed and anointed himself" (verse 20). While the child was sick, David refused to bathe or anoint himself. He wore all the signs of a man in grief, much like a widow wears black at her husband's funeral—but when they told him the child had died, *The End* scrolled across the screen of his mind. He decided then and there not to allow the tragedy to dictate the terms of his future.

May I meddle a bit again? *Why are you still wearing that long, sad face? Why will you still not venture beyond your four walls and enjoy life again?* These are overused, worn-out, stale signs of grief that need to be buried. Whatever it was, it's over. You must now get over *it*! Begin today to remove all outward signs of your "passed past." Wash your face, shave (of course, if you are a man), go buy a few new clothes, make some phone calls, break out of your self-imposed prison.

Then, he worshiped God. "So David . . .went into the house of the LORD and worshiped" (verse 20). It has been said that the same sun that melts butter hardens clay. Some people allow the fire of tragedy and failure to harden their hearts toward God. They grant permission for the past to sabotage their relationship with Him. Others allow failure and pain to melt them in His presence. Hear me: It is your choice. One of the things that made David great was his beautiful ability always to turn in the direction of Jehovah. If he fell, he fell toward God. If he broke, he broke in His arms. If he melted, it was at His feet. By observing David's actions at the death of his son, I can hear him saying, "It is over, Lord. There is nothing I can do about the past. Here I am. I give You the shattered pieces of my broken life. I believe You are a God who forgives. My future is in Your hands."

David returned to life as normal. "Then he went to his own house; and when he requested, they set food before him, and he ate" (verse 20). Scripture is clear that there is "a time to mourn, and a time to dance" (Ecclesiastes 3:4). Not that David was dancing, but the time for mourning was over. Life had to go on. I see David refusing to allow the dark trappings of perpetually self-punishing condemnation to wrap tentacles around his soul. *He moved on.* This does not mean he was unfeeling; he simply realized that it was over. He let *The End* come to an end so that he could step into a new beginning.

David's servants were puzzled by his actions: "You fasted and wept for the child while he was alive, but when the child died, you arose and ate food" (2 Samuel 12:21). In other words, they were saying, "What's the deal? Where is the expected acceleration of grief now that he is gone?"

David explained his reasoning this way: "While the child was alive, I fasted and wept; for I said, 'Who can tell whether the LORD will be gracious to me, that the child may live?'" (verse 22). He was saying, "While there was still a chance, I did all I could. I gave it my best shot. I kept hope alive." Then he continued: "But now he is dead; why should I fast? Can I bring him back again?" (verse 23). Oh, friend, we need to hear this. *You do what you can do until there is nothing more you can do.* If it does not work, *it's over.*

Do you recall our discussion of this very issue in chapter 3? You cannot resurrect something that is forever gone. David admitted, "I can't bring him back." You may not be able to bring back that job, marriage, child, church, reputation or any number of things you long to reclaim, but God can still do a new thing! The key is not to ask endlessly, "Why?" but rather, "What now? What is the answer?" For David, it was to rise, put off the signs of mourning, break toward God, worship Him and then return to life as normal. *It was time to move on.* Finally, David placed the finishing touch on a masterful response during a time of crisis.

He left all in God's hands. "I shall go to him [the child], but he shall not return to me" (verse 23). There is something beautifully abandoning in that statement. The famous Serenity Prayer comes to mind: "God, grant me the serenity to accept the things I cannot change; courage to change the things I can; and wisdom to know the difference." David had the wisdom to know what could and could not be changed, and so must all those seeking to leave the past behind. If you cannot change it, move on. If you can change it, by all means do—but above all, *know the difference.*

By the way, though the child's death was a tragedy, David's confidence that he would "go to him" forever settles the debate over what happens to children who are short-circuited into eternity. One day, dear bereaved parent, you will go to him or her in that place where all tears are wiped away and sorrow is no more (see Revelation 21:4).

The Challenge Is Answered

Now, let's return to Israel and how she responded to the ringing challenge to turn to a new day. What did the Israelites do? History tells us that thousands of them did indeed leave their past behind. They walked through the door opening miraculously before them and moved back to their homeland. Yet, tragically, many thousands more stayed in the land of their captivity. We call them the *diaspora*, meaning "that which is sown." The word applies to Jews living outside of Palestine and maintaining their religious faith among the Gentiles. In its description of this word, *The New Unger's Bible Dictionary* (Moody, 1957) tells us: "The 'ten tribes' never returned at all from [the earlier Assyrian] captivity, neither must the return of the tribes of Judah and Benjamin [from Babylon] be conceived of as complete."

Think about that for a moment. Of all who were taken captive, only a faithful minority returned. The majority simply could not transition from bound to free, from captive to liberated, from people of the past to people of the future. The Babylonian captives did not obey Isaiah's prophetic word. Settling for life in the land of bondage, these people allowed a defeated past to rob them of the "new thing" God was doing.

The minority who dared to move on, however, rebuilt Jerusalem, the Temple and their lives. They thrived in the epicenter of God's will. When someone told them, "The captivity is over," they believed it and walked through the door marked "The End." *The End* heralded a new beginning for them. I call them the *It's over* crowd. A failed past, bondages and regrets were behind them. *The End.*

Are you ready to let *over* be *over* and step into what is already sprouting up for you? If so, excellent! In the following chapter we are going to look at a few things you can expect in light of your decision. It is time for a crossing. The road is probably going to harbor some pitfalls and may prove to be a bit bumpy. But take heart, for "He who is in you is greater than he who is in the world" (1 John 4:4).

Points to Ponder

1. Are you currently facing the door marked *The End* and struggling to walk through it? If so, what are you afraid will happen if you do? Is that fear valid?
2. Is it hard for you to imagine that God is preparing something beautiful on the other side of your letting go? If so, why? If not, can you see blessings already sprouting up around you?

Crossings

He said to them, "Let us cross over to the other side."

Mark 4:35

Don't be afraid to go out on a limb. That's where the fruit is.

Anonymous

Once "it's over" is settled, you are free to begin your journey to what God has in store for you. While you no doubt now recognize Jesus as Savior, healer and deliverer, I want you to think of Him for a moment as the *Lord of crossings*. A quick scan of Scripture reveals that much of the ministry of Christ involved "carrying" people from one place to another. From sickness to health, death to life, blindness to sight, insanity to sanity, despair to hope and, I might add, *out of the past and into the future*. Jesus' ministry was earmarked by escorting people from point *A* to point *B*.

The Bible is a handbook for travelers who are in the process of making a crossing. It informs us that we are

While you no doubt now recognize Jesus as Savior, healer and deliverer, I want you to think of Him for a moment as the *Lord of crossings.*

only journeying through this world. Ultimately, we are *crossing over* from earth to heaven. The men and women held up in Scripture as our earthly examples possessed a "crossing" mindset. The writer of Hebrews tells us, "These men of faith I have mentioned died without ever receiving all that God had promised them; but they saw it all awaiting them on ahead and were glad, for they agreed that *this earth was not their real home* but that they were just strangers visiting down here. And quite obviously when they talked like that, they were looking forward to their real home in heaven" (Hebrews 11:13–14, TLB, emphasis added).

If you spend much time studying Scripture you, too, will come away with a "just passing through" mentality. Peter said that you should "spend the time of your stay here on earth with reverent fear" (1 Peter 1:17, PHILLIPS). I cannot read the words *time of your stay* without hearing an echo from those who were mentioned in Hebrews: *The earth is not my home.* Planet earth is more like a hotel where we live out the "time of our stay," and then move on. Soon we will cross over from one residence to another. Though we have not yet arrived, one thing is certain—*this is not it.*

And one day soon the Lord of crossings will execute His "coup de grace" when He returns to rapture His Church from earth to heaven. What a magnificent crossing that will be! In an instant our mortal bodies will put on immortality as we cross from earth to heaven, *in a moment, in the twinkling of an eye* (see 1 Corinthians 15:52). As His Church we wait in quiet expectation for the *Lord of crossings* to initiate the greatest crossing of all time!

In the meantime, it is very much like Jesus to bid us cross to the other side of *somewhere*—not just from earth to heaven, but also from a point *A* to a point *B in this lifetime.*

Wherever "somewhere" happens to be depends on our individual walks—what He is calling us to do, and what He wants to accomplish in our spiritual growth. He beckons us to leave the familiar shore, helps us to make our crossing and then places us in our new destination. We are not called to stagnation but to ongoing progress.

Think about this: Isn't it in the context of a crossing that our salvation begins? A crossing from death to life, lost to found and darkness to light marks the new birth. In an instant we cross the great chasm of being objects of wrath to objects of mercy: "But because of his great love for us, God . . . made us *alive* with Christ even when we were *dead* in transgressions" (Ephesians 2:4–5, NIV, emphasis added). The very first time we come into contact with Christ it is in the context of a crossing. After our first encounter we discover that He becomes the Lord of many more crossings in this life.

As we are learning, Jesus calls us to walk away from unfruitful attachments to the past so that we can step into the future He has for us. Remember Paul's pattern: "*Forgetting* the past and looking forward to what lies ahead" (Philippians 3:13, TLB, emphasis added). It is impossible to strain toward what is ahead without first letting go of the past. Then and only then are we free to make our crossings to the next level. He calls us *out of* one thing so that He might bring us *into* another. He bids us *depart* that we might *arrive*.

Have you noticed, as I have, that Jesus extends appealing "enticements" for us to make the journey? As already mentioned, sometimes He reveals a promise of what awaits. Who can possibly read the fantastic Technicolor descriptions of heaven in the book of Revelation without wanting to go there someday? Images of streets of gold winding their way through an environment where death, sorrow, crying and pain no longer exist are incredibly compelling (see Revelation 21:4). How many millions of people facing the final, great crossing through the valley of the shadow of

Who can possibly read the fantastic Technicolor descriptions of heaven in the book of Revelation without wanting to go there someday?

death have not been heartened by these verses describing the other side?

Listen to Jesus' comforting words: "Let not your heart be troubled. You are trusting God, now trust in me. There are many homes up there where my Father lives, and I am going to prepare them for your coming" (John 14:1–2, TLB). Is it not the promise of a heaven on the other side that has helped motivate millions upon millions to receive Christ? A Gospel that promises me a ticket to such an incredible place of glory via the shed blood of Jesus Christ is irresistible. Then Jesus placed a cherry on top of the sundae: "I will come and get you, so that you can always be with me where I am" (verse 3, TLB). The Lord of crossings will one day come again, take our hands and lead us across to the other side!

In other places we are tantalized with promises that build our expectations; we are not unlike children waiting excitedly to open gifts on Christmas morning: "No eye has seen, no ear has heard, no mind has conceived what God has prepared for those who love him" (1 Corinthians 2:9, NIV). I do not know exactly what awaits us on the other side, but, boy, does that verse spike my curiosity! My eyes have never seen it, my ears have not heard it and my mind has not imagined it, so it must be incredible. Consider John's statement: "We can't even imagine what it is going to be like later on. But we do know this, that when he comes we will be like him, as a result of seeing him as he really is" (1 John 3:2, TLB). We cannot imagine it because it is *unimaginable.*

But what about the *here and now*? When Jesus calls us to step into His boat for a journey from point *A* to point *B*, are there still surprises waiting? Is it worth the journey? If so, what can we expect to find? Upon relinquishing our visual grip on the rearview mirror, what do we

Crossings mean testing. And they are designed to equip us for what we will need on our arrival to the other side.

see as we peer down the road through the windshield of faith and hope? Let us explore a few different aspects of "crossings" as revealed in the Bible, for they are especially important to gaining an understanding of this principle of looking forward with expectancy.

Hang On, It's Going to Be a Bumpy Ride!

In Mark's gospel alone, Jesus is recorded to have "crossed over" the Sea of Galilee five separate times. If you were His follower, you were going to encounter some crossings . . . *guaranteed*. In three of the five crossings it appears the disciples went along for the ride voluntarily. In the other two they were *commanded* to cross over—once with Him asleep on a cushion in the stern, and another time without Him in the boat at all (see Mark 4:35; 6:45). It is interesting that in both of these crossings the disciples encountered adversity: In one, a sudden, vicious storm blew across the sea, and in the other, a "contrary wind" arose that made all the strongest efforts seem in vain.

These two episodes reveal spiritual truths that we can apply to our real-life crossings from the past into what lies ahead. We are going to study them in more detail in the next chapter, but for now we glean this important lesson: *Crossings mean testing. And they are designed to equip us for what we will need on our arrival to the other side.* The storm the disciples encountered in the first crossing was sudden, ferocious and more than a little frightening: "But soon a terrible storm arose. High waves began to break into the boat until it was nearly full of water and about to sink." Scripture says of the disciples: "Frantically they wakened him, shouting, 'Teacher, don't you even care that we are all about to drown?'" (see Mark 4:37–38, TLB).

You probably know the rest of the story. Jesus stood up, rebuked the wind and waves, and the storm ceased. At this moment it began to dawn on the Twelve exactly whom they were following. We continue in verse 41: "And they were filled with awe and said among themselves, 'Who is this man, that even the winds and seas obey him?'" The answer, of course, was simple. *He was not an ordinary man.*

In the second crossing, Jesus stayed on shore while the disciples shoved off, and then He departed to the mountain to pray (see Mark 6:45–49). As the Twelve made their way across the sea, they encountered a strong, resisting wind. Scripture records they were "rowing hard and struggling against the wind and waves" (verse 48, TLB). You have no doubt experienced the feeling of "rowing hard" and yet getting nowhere. As the spray pelted their faces and they struggled to steady the reeling boat, frustration surely entered their thoughts: *Didn't Jesus tell us to do this? Why isn't it easier? Why do we have to fight against this maddening wind?*

Finally, Jesus, who had been observing their struggle from the shore, came toward them in the fourth watch of the night (around three A.M.), walking on the sea. As the eerie silhouette approached, the Bible records the disciples' reactions: "When they saw something walking along beside them they screamed in terror, thinking it was a ghost" (verse 49, TLB). Jesus immediately spoke a word of comfort to them: "It is I! Don't be afraid" (verse 50, TLB), and He proceeded to climb into the boat. I love Mark's description of their stunned reaction to this incredible display of power over natural law: "They just sat there, unable to take it in!" (verse 51, TLB). Keep these two crossings in mind, for they illustrate powerful and pivotal truths. We will return to them for a much closer look in the next chapter.

For now, let's focus on this point: As with all crossings, when we make the decision to follow Christ out of the past there is *always a struggle.* You can count on it. The resolve to leave familiar shores in order to reach for what waits on the other side will be tried by storms of some sort. It may be a strong wind that suddenly tosses your little boat about violently, or it might be a strong, steady wind that weakens your resolve to keep going. Whichever the case, your decision to let go of what is behind you in order to reach for your destiny will at times be a bumpy journey. Do not let it take you by surprise! First Peter 4:12 encourages us: "Dear friends, don't be bewildered or surprised when you go through the fiery trials ahead, for this is no strange, unusual thing that is going to happen to you" (TLB).

Crossings take us from faith to faith, strength to strength and revelation to revelation.

As we will discover in this chapter, crossings are defining seasons from which we emerge stronger, wiser and more capable of spiritual fruitfulness. Once on the other side of a crossing, we are never quite the same. They grow us up, enhance our knowledge of God and precede spiritual promotion, which is why both God and our enemy care so much about them. Each time that firm whisper from the Carpenter of Nazareth can be heard calling us to "cross over to the other side," we can be certain an exciting new day is around the corner! As we explore the following examples, we will uncover principles for our own journeys out of the past.

Abraham's Crossing: Into the Unknown

Scripture is replete with stories of historic crossings that, for good or bad, proved to be defining moments. Let's begin with the story of Abram, whom God later renamed Abraham. God gave him this command: "Get out of your country, from your family and from your father's house, to a land that I will show you" (Genesis 12:1). The father of our faith obeyed by leaving his comfort zone (house, family and familiar surroundings) and traveling to a far-off land. Each

The goal is not just to reach the other side, but more importantly, to *become* whom God intends us to become during the journey.

step of the four-hundred-mile journey from Ur of the Chaldees to Shechem, the first leg of his trip, echoed with faith. Not only did he cross hundreds of miles of unknown territory, but he also crossed the great river Euphrates.

Abram's future greatness hinged on making these momentous crossings. Listen closely to God's promise: "I will make you a great nation; I will bless you and make your name great. . . . And in you all the families of the earth shall be blessed" (verses 2–3). All of the "I will"s of God's promise hinged on Abram leaving the familiar shores of Ur and crossing into the land God would show him. Literally, this says: *no crossing, no greatness.* Crossings mold greatness into our character. The goal is not just to reach the other side, but more importantly, to *become* whom God intends us to become during the journey.

As he journeyed, Abram became intimate with God as well as His ways. To say that his crossing was merely a scenic trek through beautiful Middle Eastern countryside would be a gross misrepresentation. The father of our faith encountered testing, temptation, doubts and trials. He learned what God blesses, and he also learned what provokes the Father's rebukes. God showed Abram in no uncertain terms, for instance, that he did not have to hide behind lies in order to protect himself (see Genesis 12:10–20). In the crucible of heartbreak and regret, he learned that he did not have to "help God out" by stepping into the flesh in order to bring His will to pass (see Genesis 16). Abram bore successes and failures, ups and downs. Yet through it all, he became the father of our faith, the father of many nations—Abraham—during the process of crossing over.

For me, the lesson learned from Abraham's crossing is that of trusting God with *unknown outcomes.* Abraham faced many unknowns, but he learned to trust the hands of a sovereign God to shape his future. Here are a few of the unknowns that built his faith:

- Abraham did not know where his journey would take him. "Get out of your country . . . to a land that I will show you" (Genesis 12:1). God's proposition was, "If you will, I will."
- When in a land dispute with his nephew Lot, he left the outcome of which parcel he would possess in the hands of God. He said to Lot: "Please let there be no strife between you and me. . . . Is not the whole land before you? Please separate from me. If you take the left, then I will go to the right; or, if you go to the right, then I will go to the left" (Genesis 13:8–9). Lot chose the luscious land that comprised Sodom and Gomorrah, and Abraham dwelt in the land of Canaan.
- Abraham willingly offered Isaac, not knowing how God would work in the life of this child of promise. Only by the intervention of an angel did Abraham refrain from sacrificing his son. "But the Angel of the Lord called to him from heaven. . . . And He said, 'Do not lay your hand on the lad.' . . . Then Abraham lifted his eyes and . . . behind him was a ram caught in a thicket by its horns" (Genesis 22:11–13).

As we continue our journey, we will find that the broad view through the windshield holds many surprising twists and turns, for unknown factors are part of any journey of faith. With Paul we can readily say, "For now we see through a glass, darkly" (1 Corinthians 13:12, kjv). Thus, if we are to cross over to the other side, we must learn to trust God with the outcome. As with Abraham, it is only as we continue in obedience that the unknown becomes known. If we do not complete the crossing, what *would have been* remains hidden.

Israel's Crossing: Un-Renewed Minds

God raised up Moses to prepare an entire nation for a historic crossing. After Egypt suffered the effects of ten horrible plagues, Pharaoh finally released the children of Israel to go serve their own God. Scripture reveals that Israel was called to undertake three major crossings in order to reach the Promised Land—the Red Sea, the wilderness and the Jordan River. Through the first two challenges, they would learn that crossings challenge the way we think. The third challenge, crossing the Jordan River, taught a different lesson and will be discussed in the next section, "Joshua's Crossing."

The first challenge, the Red Sea, came on the heels of the Israelites' deliverance from Egypt (see Exodus 14). Here, the entire nation seemed to face an impossible predicament. A wide, flowing sea blocked the way before them and Pharaoh's angry army approached swiftly behind them. Doubts of God's eternal care filled their hearts when they cried to Moses, "Because there were no graves in Egypt, have you taken us away to die in the wilderness?" (verse 11). It is interesting that these words have a certain echo in the story of Jesus' disciples trying to cross the Sea of Galilee with the storm blowing wildly about them: "Don't You care that we perish?" God always cares, of course, much more than they—or we—can imagine. For the Israelites, the challenge at the Red Sea to grasp God's view of them was their first class in the school of crossings: "Promised Land Preparation 101."

The next crossing was also designed to help them see themselves and their faith, but it took a different approach. The Red Sea crossing was intended to deliver them *from* Egypt and all that it represented, such as slavery and hopelessness. The wilderness crossing, on the other hand, was intended to remove Egypt *from them*. While they had departed from Egypt *geographically*, Egypt's influence still remained in their hearts. Their first crossing was a success, but the second crossing was a tragic failure.

Still, an important point was made: *Successful crossings always qualify us to make our next one.* Crossing the Red Sea qualified the Israelites to enter the wilderness. If they had crossed the wilderness successfully they would have been ready to cross the Jordan River, and then finally to enter the Promised Land.

Successful crossings always qualify us to make our next one.

What held this God-ordained nation, so full of potential, back for forty long years of frustration and futility? They did not allow their minds to focus ahead on the next crossing. For starters, they wanted to linger in the past. (Remember chapter 2?) When faced with hardship, these people of promise quickly adjusted the rearview mirror and looked back: "And the children of Israel said to them, 'Oh, that we had died by the hand of the LORD in the land of Egypt, when we sat by the pots of meat and when we ate bread to the full!'" (Exodus 16:3).

This complaint was, of course, poppycock. Their misery index had been off the charts in Egypt. When God called to Moses out of the burning bush, He described their condition: "I have surely seen the oppression of My people who are in Egypt, and have heard their cry because of their taskmasters, for I know their sorrows" (Exodus 3:7). Oppression, crying, taskmasters and sorrow: These words do not paint a picture of a bounteous vacation spot! Yet, incredibly, Israel fell into a double trap. They not only lingered in the past, they falsely romanticized it. (Remember chapter 3?) In order to cross the wilderness successfully, they needed to release the past and focus on the Promised Land.

The lesson learned from Israel's failure to cross the wilderness is that *stinking thinking can hinder forward progress.* From the onset, Israel's biggest enemy was herself. Lack of water, predictable manna or the giants they spied on the other side did not have the power to take her down. The Israelites did that themselves; they proved to be their own worst enemies. Listen carefully: *Crossings come to change us.* They reveal flaws in our thinking and motivate us to renew our minds so that we can make it to the other side. If we are to "cross over" successfully from the past into the future, we must not allow negative, defeatist thinking to rob us of victory.

Our own issues can blur the view through the windshield. That is why we must consistently pull over, grab the Word of God and allow it to wash away the dirt that blocks our vision.

Joshua's Crossing: Obedience

Again, we find in Scripture that a crossing of some sort often precedes fresh beginnings, new horizons and divine promotion. Entering the Promised Land was no different. The children of the wilderness wanderers had watched mom and dad miss the Promised Land, and they did not want to die in the wilderness as they had: "With most of them [that earlier generation] God was not well pleased, for their bodies were scattered in the wilderness" (1 Corinthians 10:5). Hence, Joshua took great pains to prepare the second generation to cross over. He told them, "Prepare provisions for yourselves, for within three days you will cross over this Jordan, to go in to possess the land" (Joshua 1:11).

After giving further instructions (see Joshua 3:1–4), Joshua closed by telling them why obedience was so crucial: "For you have not passed this way before" (verse 4). As we saw with Abraham, crossings usually involve the unknown. The second generation was about to journey to a new place in a new manner. Notice the word *passed* in verse 4 above. *Passed*, according to Strong's *Concordance*, comes from the Hebrew word *`abar*, meaning "to cross over, go over, go beyond, get over, go through, pass through, and pass beyond." Another of its meanings is "to pass from one side to the other side." An important derivative of *`abar* is the word *`ibri*, meaning "Hebrew." And *Hebrew*, of course, is the ethnic description of Abraham and his descendants. So the Hebrew race was named after a word meaning "to cross over from one side to the other side." Our spiritual ancestors, along with the father of our faith, were created to be renowned as "those who crossed over."

What does all this mean for us? When God requires us as His children to cross over from a bad habit to wholeness, stagnation to fruitfulness, from insecurity to a walk of faith—from point *A* to point *B*—it is in our spiritual bloodline to obey Him and cross over! Our spiritual ancestors have already traveled there before us. As it was with the disciples of Jesus and the fathers of Israel before them, conflict and difficulties may accompany you on your journey. Storms and resisting winds may push against you on the way. Nevertheless, Jesus, the *Lord of crossings*, will see you safely to the other side.

It is extremely significant that Joshua instructed the people to wait until the Ark of the Covenant, carried by the priests, passed one thousand yards in front of them. The Ark was Israel's most sacred possession, representing the very presence of God. The distance was required so that Israel would not forget its sacredness. As they say, familiarity breeds contempt.

The contents of the Ark, by the way, were most significant. First, there was manna, which represented God as provider. Then there was Aaron's rod, representing God's authority. And finally, the Ark contained the Ten Commandments, the very Word of God.

When God calls us to make a crossing out of the past to what lies ahead, this Old Testament picture presents a mighty spiritual truth. We must keep Jesus, the Ark of the

New Covenant, sacred in our hearts, never forgetting to show Him the reverence that is due. We must also never forget that He is our provider, our authority and the very Word of God. In any step of faith we must hold close to these truths, because wherever the crossing takes us we can be assured that we "have not passed this way before."

Reminiscent of the parting of the Red Sea under Moses' leadership, as soon as the priests' feet dipped into the Jordan's cold, muddy waters, "the waters which came down from upstream stood still" (Joshua 3:16). The children of the first generation wilderness wanderers walked across on dry ground and stepped onto the coveted Promised Land.

The lesson we can learn from Joshua's crossing is that of *victory through obedience*. As already mentioned, the second generation was not about to repeat their parents' mistakes. They did exactly what Joshua told them to do. No complaining, murmuring or outspoken wishes to return to Egypt could be heard. Silently and obediently they crossed into the vast, unexplored inheritance God had promised to Abraham centuries before.

Through unknown outcomes, the trap of stinking thinking and on to victory through obedience, crossings carry us to the distant shore of a new day. Anticipation builds as we sense the stir of faith deep in our souls, and the fresh, exhilarating atmosphere of a place we have never been before.

Points to Ponder

1. As you have sensed God's call to turn from the rear-view mirror, what has your response been? Are you fearful? Excited?
2. If you were to describe your present crossing, would you say that you are handling the test of *uncertain outcomes* well? What about dealing with *stinking thinking*? Are you experiencing *victory through obedience*?

On the Other Side

Then they came to the other side of the sea.

Mark 5:1

Just one act of yours may turn the tide of another person's life.

Anonymous

Imagine for a moment a sea of faces. You do not know them and they do not know you. At least . . . *not yet*. As you survey the crowd you notice that some of them are very sad. Others wear lines of worry and stress on their tired faces. Still others seem perplexed. One group appears to be defeated, their strength gone, their hope dried up. As the faces come into view your heart goes out to them. Who are these people? If you look into the Scriptures you can solve this riddle. *They are the ones waiting on the other side of your crossing.*

Part of the reason you have passed through all that you have is to prepare you to touch the lives of others. A divine

Every experience with God is like a baton you hand off to someone else in the race of life.

encounter is in store for you and those whose paths you have been destined to cross. Each time He strengthened you, taught you and carried you through a crossing, *God had them in mind.* They are living proof that you were created to be an answer, not a question mark. Many of the issues they face will remain unsettled until you step onto your new shore and greet them.

It took a while for me to realize that God's dealings in my private life were not only *about* or *for* me. *Others* were in His mind. Read the following verse slowly: "[He] comforts us in all our troubles, so that we can comfort those in any trouble with the comfort we ourselves have received from God" (2 Corinthians 1:4, NIV). God comforts us in all of our troubles *so that* we can, in turn, comfort others who are also in trouble.

You cannot give what you do not have, but you will always give what you *do* have. Just as troubled people *trouble* people, if you are a *healed* person, you will bring healing to others. Each experience is like a baton you hand off to someone else in the race of life.

Who can help the heartbroken more successfully than someone who has fought through equal heartbreak and crossed over into a new beginning? Who has a stronger arm with which to pull the fallen out of the pit of despair than someone who has climbed back from crippling failure? Who is more effective in helping the traumatized move on from paralyzing memories than someone who has learned to turn from the past and face the dawn of a new day? And who better to navigate the embittered through the struggle of forgiveness than those who were once slammed to the mat by an offense?

After walking with Christ for many years, I realize that through all our ups and downs, victories and defeats, *God is giving us a testimony.* There is nothing that overcomes the work of the devil like someone who can say, "I was trapped in the past as the result of wounding and pain, but He brought me out into a brand-new beginning."

Testimonies are diamonds developed in the intense pressure of trials. They are pearls formed when irritating grains of sand lodge within unhappy oysters.

John talked about the power of a testimony when he said: "They [the brethren] defeated him [the accuser] by the blood of the Lamb, and by their testimony" (Revelation 12:11, TLB). The Twelve, of course, saw Jesus *personally* and witnessed His power. Some years later, Peter declared: "My own eyes have seen his splendor and his glory" (2 Peter 1:16, TLB). John also proclaimed: "I myself have seen him with my own eyes and listened to him speak. I have touched him with my own hands. He is God's message of Life" (1 John 1:1, TLB). They were enormously effective in their witness for Christ because of their experiences. In addition, Luke wrote about the importance of these personal stories in keeping authentic records of Christ's work on earth: "Many have undertaken to draw up an account of the things that have been fulfilled among us, just as they were handed down to us by those who from the first were eyewitnesses" (Luke 1:1–2, NIV).

And still we, today, witness His power. God is ever looking to bring you through a problem, not only to bless you, but to give you a testimony also so that you might say, "With my own eyes I have seen His power to deliver." Testimonies are diamonds developed in the intense pressure of trials. They are pearls formed when irritating grains of sand lodge within unhappy oysters. Testimonies are rainbows after the storm, springtime after a harsh winter. A testimony rings with truth like a bell in the souls of those seeking the reality of God. Granted, there is no testimony without a "test" and some "moaning"—but once you pass through it you possess something that can bring defeat to a satanic assignment in the life of another.

Preparing for What's Ahead

Let's return now to the disciples' two journeys across the Sea of Galilee. In the first crossing they learned that Jesus was not just a charismatic leader, powerful speaker, healer and deliverer. The Twelve were broadsided with the growing realization that Jesus was God. No wonder they exclaimed, "Who ever can he be?—even the wind and the waves do what he tells them!" (Mark 4:41, PHILLIPS). The trail of their astonished thoughts could lead to only one conclusion: Who but God would have power over wind and waves? Who else could command a fierce storm to stop its roaring, as if He were soothing a crying baby?

Following this crossing, the Twelve landed on the shores of Gadara. Out of the graveyard a man possessed by demons appeared and ran toward them. Mark records: "Immediately there met Him out of the tombs a man with an unclean spirit" (Mark 5:2). It is difficult to imagine the horror of the scene that greeted them. In fact, in all the annals of demon possession, this was a uniquely evil and unnerving case. Matthew Henry writes, "The devil is a cruel master. This wretched creature was night and day in the mountains and in the tombs, crying, and cutting himself with stones."

The Gadarene demoniac was free to wander about, for no earthly restraint could subdue him. Possessing supernatural strength, he snapped iron chains as though they were made of twigs. The pitifully possessed man ran about naked, though covered in self-inflicted wounds, and lived in the neighborhood graveyard. Like a great, frightening ogre he blocked the entrance to the town "so that no one could pass that way" (Matthew 8:28). He was a poster boy for what Satan does to those he enslaves. Seeing Jesus from a distance, the

The Twelve needed to understand, on a deeper level than ever, who Jesus really was. It was one thing to tell them timeless truths but entirely another to have show-and-tell!

demoniac ran and fell at His feet, while foreign voices began to speak out of him declaring that they were "legion." A Roman legion of that day numbered six thousand men. The word *legion* had come to signify a well-organized group possessing great power. At this juncture any normal man would have fled in terror!

Let us pause a moment and recall what the disciples had just learned. Remember their astonished response following Jesus' stilling of the storm? "Even the wind and the sea obey Him!" (Mark 4:41). In other words, no storm is beyond the calming touch of Jesus. Do you think that lesson jumped into their minds as they looked at this pathetic soul from their destined sea of faces? Of course it did! If the howling winds and stormy sea submitted to His command to be still, if nature itself bowed to His authority, then the hideous storm inside this man would bow, too.

Keep in mind what they were learning—that Jesus was God in fleshly form. John, writing years later, informs us in no uncertain terms, "The Word [Jesus] *was God*" (John 1:1, emphasis added). Our triune God possesses three characteristics unique to Him alone: He is omnipresent (everywhere at once), omniscient (all-knowing) and omnipotent (all-powerful). *He is God.* He is *never* surprised or taken aback by anything. When Jesus embarked with them across the sea, for instance, He knew full well that a storm was coming. Why, then, did He allow them to experience it? Why did He not speak to the storm while it lurked in the distance, far away from the little fishing boat? *The Twelve needed to understand, on a deeper level than ever, who He really was.* It was one thing to tell them timeless truths but entirely another to have show-and-tell!

Can you see now that the disciples' crossing on that momentous journey taught them what they would need to know

He could sleep only because he had a few crossings behind him, during which he learned what we might call the eleventh commandment—*Thou shalt not sweat it.*

for the challenges and demands to be encountered on the other side? The Gadarene demoniac was not staring wild-eyed at normal men with typical life experiences. He encountered twelve individuals who had watched firsthand as the Lord of the universe stopped a life-threatening storm by simply telling it to be still. While the demoniac was frighteningly supernatural in his physical strength, *he was no match for Jesus*, who was supremely supernatural in His divine power. Rather than evidence of terror in their eyes, the disciples looked with fresh faith toward the one who had brought them across the waters.

Their faith proved to be well placed. Jesus took total control over the angry horde of devils possessing the tormented man. The demon spirits literally asked permission of Christ to enter a herd of swine. He granted it. "The herd ran violently down the steep place into the sea, and drowned in the sea" (Mark 5:13). Just as the storm at sea had been replaced with "a great calm," the man who had terrorized an entire town was soon found "sitting and clothed and in his right mind" (verse 15).

The wide-eyed disciples sailed from Gadara with a truth they never forgot. *There was not a crisis on earth Jesus could not handle.* He was Lord over every storm, impossibility and dilemma. No wonder we find Simon Peter years later sleeping away in a jail cell the night before he was to face an angry mob and possibly execution. (Hmm, sleeping in a storm. Does this remind you of someone else?) "Peter was sleeping, bound with two chains between two soldiers" (Acts 12:6). How could he sleep at a time like that? I maintain he could sleep only because he had a few crossings behind him, during which he learned what we might call the eleventh commandment—*Thou shalt not sweat it.*

Preparing for Something Bigger

It is important to take note of what preceded the second crossing. Jesus had been teaching a great crowd numbering in the thousands. The Bible says that there were five thousand men, so we must assume that at least that many women and children were there. The gospel of Mark tells us that He was "moved with compassion" for them, for they were "like sheep not having a shepherd" (Mark 6:34).

As the day grew late they became hungry. The disciples suggested to Jesus that He "send them away, that they may go into the surrounding country and villages and buy themselves bread" (verse 36). Christ responded by making an absurd suggestion: "You give them something to eat" (verse 37). He might as well have told them to fly to the moon! Understandably, the disciples responded by asking if they should go and buy hundreds of dollars' worth of bread. That is when Jesus asked how much food was among them. "Five loaves and two fishes," they responded (see verse 38). That was all He needed. He took that meager amount, blessed it, broke it and distributed it to the people. Amazingly, the more food the disciples handed out, the more it multiplied. I like to say that it was the original "Wonder Bread."

This was an astounding miracle. When it was all said and done, twelve basketfuls were left over, one for each disciple. Upwards of ten thousand people were fed from virtually nothing. If I let my imagination run wild, I picture the disciples around the halfway point just starting to laugh out loud at the sheer awesomeness of what was happening. *What else could they do?* They would stick their hand in a basket, take out bread and then watch it supernaturally reappear.

Now, let's put that story on the back burner and move on to the second crossing. The Bible says, "Immediately He made His disciples get into the boat and go before Him to the other side, to Bethsaida, while He sent the

This is the stuff of crossings. Unexpected, atypical, supernatural, faith-stretching, logic-bending, life-changing lessons are encountered when God wants to prepare us for something bigger.

multitude away" (verse 45). This time Jesus stayed on shore while the disciples shoved off to sea. We are told Christ then "departed to the mountain to pray" (verse 46).

As the Twelve made their way across the sea, they encountered a strong, resisting wind. Scripture records that they were "rowing hard and struggling against the wind and waves" (verse 46, TLB). You have no doubt experienced the sense of "rowing hard" and getting nowhere yourself. It is the pits. When frustration from human effort reached the boiling point, Jesus—who had been observing their struggle from the shore—"came to them, walking on the sea" (verse 48). Again, this happened in the middle of the night.

I am repeating parts of this scene because words cannot do justice to this incredible picture. When they saw the form of Jesus approaching on the water, the disciples thought they were seeing a ghost and cried out in terror (see verse 49). What a day that had been! First, they had witnessed the unexplainable multiplication of fish and loaves, and now a ghost was walking toward them, gliding effortlessly across the rolling waves.

This is the stuff of crossings. Unexpected, atypical, supernatural, faith-stretching, logic-bending, life-changing lessons are encountered when God wants to prepare us for something bigger. Crossings invariably introduce us to a side of God we have not formerly known. It is in the context of crossings that He steps into our little box of understanding, that place in our minds where we file away our preconceived notions of who He is, and kicks the sides out. I can just hear the disciples saying, "Uh, Jesus, would You mind just being a good, cookie-cutter Savior? Just make life a little easier for us, and cut out all the theatrics? You are scaring us!"

Jesus, unaffected by the inclement conditions, spoke words of comfort to them and climbed into the boat. As soon as His feet touched the floorboards, "the wind ceased" (verse 51). That is when Mark gave that excellent description of the disciples' stunned reactions to this incredible display of power over natural law. They were unable to take it in. Where I come from we call this the "deer in the headlights" stare.

The purpose of this second crossing was first, of course, a natural one. They needed to reach Bethsaida where more of the sea of faces awaited their arrival. It was also a repeat lesson. Mark tells us there was one reason the disciples were so totally blown away by Christ's trek across the water: "They had not understood about the loaves, because their heart was hardened" (verse 52).

In the first crossing, the disciples began to grasp the idea that this Jesus was God; the one who calmed the storm also calmed the raging heart of the demoniac. But they still did not understand the magnitude of Jesus' power and goodness; "their heart was hardened." If they had grasped what He intended them to learn when He multiplied the loaves, they would not have been surprised at His ability to walk on the water. It was as if Christ were saying:

> "Guys, you simply have to understand whom you are walking with if you are going to have any impact on *your* sea of faces. *To make a big impact you must have a big God.* The whole reason I waited on the shore while you struggled and strained was to show you that, in your hour of need, I can walk on top of the very thing that troubles you! I am God. Do you get it now? I hope so, because as soon as we reach the other side we are going to be greeted by a sea of faces. We will be traveling from town to town and will be met by people straining in their attempts to 'row' through life. They are going to carry their sick and dying out into the streets. They do not need a cookie-cutter Savior. They need a miracle-working, need-meeting, life-saving, on-top-of-their-problems Messiah! Are you ready? Behold, we are nearing the shore. They come. . . ."

Would the disciples ever finally understand? The Master was not subject to natural law—far from it; the laws of nature were obviously at His command. Storm at sea? The wind and waves were no hindrance to His plans. Crossing vast waters on foot? Gravity was no issue as He silently strolled across the deep, dark sea. Hopelessness? Disease? Death? No power on earth could block His mission. These revelations were not random lessons for the sake of the moment. Remember the principle of giving what you have. Everything the Twelve learned of Him in their crossings was invaluable to other people once they reached the other side. *This is the point of your "crossings" as well: Crossings are custom designed to prepare you for divine encounters with those who will be hurting just as you are.*

They Finally Got It

One day, Peter and John were making their way to the Temple to pray (see Acts 3). They had already encountered a good part of the sea of faces they were destined to touch. The fires of Pentecost were burning. Peter had preached his first sermon. Three thousand spiritually hungry people had been saved upon hearing a three-minute message. No doubt about it, *now the disciples got it—everything they had experienced with Jesus was making sense*. The crossings were all about showing them who He was.

As they were walking, a lame man sat outside the gate of the Temple and begged alms from Peter and John. "Any spare change?" he asked. We *know* Peter finally got it by what he said: "Silver and gold I do not have, but what I *do have* I give you: In the name of Jesus Christ of Nazareth, rise up and walk" (verse 6, emphasis added). That man jumped up immediately and went "walking, leaping, and praising God" (verse 8).

Peter could not give what he did not have, but he *could give* what he did have. He had a great big, miracle-working, need-meeting, life-saving, on-top-of-his-problems Messiah! And he did not want to keep the blessings to himself. We will look more closely at his life in the next chapter as we continue to explore why we should remove any obstacle, including the past, in order to reach for *the other side.*

First, though, I want to relay a story I shared in my last book, *Making It Right When You Feel Wronged.* It is a memorable, modern-day picture of holding close what we need to let go of. See if it resonates with you.

A Boy and a Ball

My son, Jeremy, played T-ball as a child. (T-ball is baseball for kids as young as five years old.) There is no pitcher. Instead, a ball is placed in a little holder in front of the batter. The fledgling player eyes it carefully, swings, hopes to connect and then runs the bases like normal baseball. As a dad, I have some wonderful memories of Jeremy's T-ball games.

One day a lasting memory was made. Jeremy's team had one point on its competitor. It was the last inning, bases were loaded, there were two outs and the other guys were up to bat. Their hitter hauled off and swatted the ball way out into left field—the best hit of the game. Every eye watched it sail toward a little fellow whose hat seemed to swallow his whole head. I did not recognize him, but T-ball in our neck of the woods did not have rigid rules—you could join at any time in the season. The "hat" saw the ball coming, ran toward it and just barely missed the game-winning catch. It plopped down in front of him, rolling right into his glove. One runner had crossed home plate already, but there was still time to throw home and tie the game. Everyone in the bleacher on our side was yelling, "Throw it! Throw it!"

To the surprise of both sides, however, the little guy pulled it close, hunkered down and held onto it like a prize trophy!

I gulped as reality hit me in the gut. He simply did not get it. He did not understand the game.

He seemed to be saying, "I have waited all afternoon for this thing, and I am not about to let go of it now." The crowd went nuts. "Throw it! Hurry! Hurry!" All to no avail. I thought our coach was going to have a coronary on the spot. The entire game hinged on this play. Moments passed and the three remaining runners crossed home plate one by one. Moans drifted from our bleacher and heads shook as the little guy in left field still clutched his prize.

About this time a tall, stately man came out of the stands and walked slowly toward him. *Dad.* His father stooped down and hugged the little fellow as he stubbornly clutched the ball. Then his dad spoke to him—and moved his hands at the same time. *Sign language.* A hush fell over the stands. "It's okay, son, give me the ball," I heard him say, as he signed the words.

Embarrassed heads bowed. The little boy looked his dad in the face; tears spilled out of his eyes, but he slowly turned over the coveted ball. I gulped as reality hit me in the gut. He simply did not get it. He did not understand the game. In his child's mind, he just wanted the ball. He did not hear the crowd. He could not—he was deaf.

Like that little boy, many Christians hold on to the gifts God gives them because they do not understand the game. They do not comprehend that what He places into their hands *is not just for them*; it is also for the sea of faces they will encounter. This is the way Christianity is supposed to work.

Yet, like that little boy, we do not hear the Scriptures resounding from the grandstands: "Freely you have received, freely give" (Matthew 10:8). In our case, lack of understanding has dulled our spiritual senses and deafened us to the voice of God.

Here is the good news. Our heavenly Father eventually walks out to us on the playing field of life, kneels down and says, "It is okay, child. I gave it to you so that you could, in turn, give it to others. Let go of it! In letting go, you will be enriched, as will those you are destined to touch." *Is He saying that to you?*

If so, if you want to reach your greatest potential, which is another reward waiting on the other side of your journey out of the past, you must let go. Let's see now how Peter learned this lesson.

Points to Ponder

1. Are you making a crossing right now? If so, can you jot down the essence of what is involved?
2. When you read about the sea of faces, did you receive fresh motivation to continue in your crossing?
3. As you approach the next shore, do you have a hunch who is waiting on the other side? What do you sense God has been teaching you that will be part of your testimony to them?

Your Greatest Potential

"You are Simon, John's son—but you shall be called Peter, the rock!"

John 1:42, TLB

Our past is not our potential.

Marilyn Ferguson

The middle-aged man's bloodshot eyes squinted into the early morning sun. Deep wrinkles were etched into his weather-beaten face, which was framed partly by a salt-and-pepper beard. Peter stood up in his wooden boat and tossed his well-worn net into the sea, as he had done so many times before, hoping for that promising tug indicating a catch. Having fished all of his life on the shores of the Sea of Galilee, he moved in rhythm with the humdrum routine of grinding out a living. Naturally good-natured, the hardy fisherman was a rugged, blue-collar worker who, I imagine,

Once
our sin debt
is settled,
He buoys our faith
by saying,
"You are a
person of
destiny."

was right at home with a good joke at the local fish fry . . . but one day all of that changed.

When Jesus was beginning to gather His future disciples, He made His first public appearance—being baptized by his cousin John (see John 1). Seeing Christ approach the Jordan River to be baptized, John declared, "Behold! The Lamb of God who takes away the sin of the world!" (verse 29). One of the first to hear Jesus speak following this event was Andrew, Simon Peter's brother. Andrew became convinced that Jesus was the long-anticipated Messiah. Deeply moved, he sought out Peter and announced, "We have found the Messiah" (verse 41). In a classic picture of New Testament witnessing, "He brought him to Jesus" (verse 42).

Jesus wasted no time in reading Peter's mail, so to speak. "'You are Simon the son of Jonah,' He said. 'You shall be called Cephas' (which is translated, A Stone)" (verse 42). Jesus' declaration to Simon was huge in its implications. *You are one thing now, but you shall be something quite different later. You have your ways, your personality, your habits, and your likes and dislikes now, but when I am finished with you, you will not be the same. I see who you are now, but I also see who you will become.*

Have you noticed that Jesus always turns our focus to what *shall be*, not what *has been*? In terms of the past, He turns our attention to the cross, where forgiveness and healing await. Once our sin debt is settled, He buoys our faith by saying, "You are a person of destiny. Let's move forward into your divine purpose." Notice how He immediately stirred hope in Peter concerning his future. *You are going to be a rock, Peter. You are significant to Me. The sky is the limit!* As the old children's song says, "You are a great big bundle of potentiality."

Who Is Defining You?

Jesus was a master at stirring the hearts of His followers with purpose. He ignited this purpose by the way He defined them. Now consider this. Right now, this very moment, *someone or something is defining you.* You believe about yourself what people or circumstances have led you to believe. Allow me to tell you something that I believe with all my heart is a key to your stepping into the future God has for you. *You must win the battle over who or what defines you.* In order to reach for the future, you must believe what God says about you. You must allow God to be the definer of who you are.

Can you see with me that Jesus set out immediately to define His future disciples? This was His groundbreaking tactic, the out-of-the-starting-gate modus operandi He employed with every single person He called. In another place, for instance, He told His future disciples, "Come after Me and be My disciples, and I will make you to *become* fishers of men" (Mark 1:17, AMP, emphasis added). Notice that He did not say, "I will teach you to fish for men." Rather, He said, "*I will make you to become.*"

The word *become* is important. According to Strong's *Concordance* it is taken from a Greek word that means "to cause to come into being." It means far more than teaching the disciples *how* to fish for men. They would be "caused to become" something they had never been before or never would become without His touch—fishers of men at heart, not just good salesmen.

Jesus defined His disciples by calling out their greatest potential. And it is the same for us. The arrow of destiny hits the bull's-eye in our souls when Christ tells us what we *shall become*. According to Psalm 42:7, deep answers to deep. From the depths of our being, a sense of knowing rises up and says, "Yes! This is what I was born for!"

This is part and parcel of the view through the windshield. No longer stuck in a foggy past, we become prime candidates for fresh purpose from a "defining" God.

The same Greek word for *become* was also used when Jesus was tempted by the devil in Matthew 4:3. The serpent hissed, "Command that these stones *become* bread" (emphasis added). Satan tempted Christ to turn the stones from one thing to something entirely different. Why would Satan tempt Him to do that? The answer is simple: The adversary knew He could.

Christ resisted the temptation to misuse His power—even though the act of turning something or someone into what that thing or that one could never be without Him is what He does best! When Jesus first spoke to Peter, He was saying, "I see your potential, and it is far beyond anything you can even begin to imagine. I am not just predicting a radical change in you; I am the one who is going to *cause you to become* what I have predicted." Translation: *Nobody can bring out your greatest potential like Me.* Christ left Peter stirred and excited about what was coming, not down and depressed over what had been. He defined him, and in defining him, He planted purpose in his heart.

This is part and parcel of the view through the windshield. No longer stuck in a foggy past, we become prime candidates for fresh purpose from a "defining" God. In light of this, consider for a moment the miracle of Peter's life. Who could have imagined in anyone's wildest dreams the person of power and influence he would one day become? *No one except Jesus.* This unknown Jewish fisherman, summoned by Christ in his middle-aged years, has gone down in history as one of the most influential human beings of all time. The thought is staggering.

Plucked from obscurity to follow Jesus from town to town for three years, Peter became one of Christ's "inner three." He was present when our Lord met with Moses and Elijah on the Mount of Transfiguration (see Mark 9:2–9). He was the only disciple to ask Christ to bid him walk on the water. Forget the fact that he started to sink; *Peter actually walked on water!* What possessed him to believe he could do that? Jesus had predicted greatness in him, and he had begun to understand the greatness of Christ. As you *believe*, you will *do*. We attempt great things when we *believe* great things.

Peter was with John when the two peered wide-eyed into the empty tomb of Christ on the first Easter morning (see John 20:3–10). Then, years following Christ's resurrection from the dead, he penned the letters we now know as 1 and 2 Peter. Have you read them lately? They are the proclamations of a theological and intellectual giant.

If you try to connect the dots from fisherman to a mighty "fisher of men," from blue-collar worker to deep-water walker, domesticated husband to pillar of the Church, and, finally, a loose-lipped braggart to a brilliant epistle writer, you will lose the trail every time. Peter cannot be explained apart from the one who said, "I will make you to *become*. . . ."

Defined by the Past

Let's recall the six chains we discussed in Part 1: inordinate attachments, past successes, heartbreak, failure, trauma and bitterness. Here is the adversary's tactic: In any way he can, with whatever method he can find, *he* wants to be the one who defines you, *and one of his favorite weapons is the past*. He uses heartbreak, failure, trauma and offenses, not just to hold you *back there*, but to define you. He conjures negative people and experiences from a bygone day in a subtle attempt to recreate an "old you," based on what may have been said or done in yesteryear. Don't you know how he must have pummeled Simon Peter following his failure during Jesus' trial and execution? You can bet that the enemy did his dead-level best to push Peter down to an even lower spiritual stature than when he had begun.

The moment you allow God to define you, your greatest potential is destined to be fulfilled.

The devil's lying words go like this: "You failed, so you *are* a failure. You were traumatized, so you *will always be* a traumatized person. You have been hurt, so you *are* doomed *to be* a hurt person, limping through life, dragging your pain behind you." Any time the enemy seeks to define you, he turns *were* into *are*. He takes an event that *was*, and personalizes it to you today. He turns the past into a mold and attempts to squeeze you into it, conforming you to its image. You *were*, so you *are*.

The moment you allow God to define you, your greatest potential is destined to be fulfilled. The truth is, I will declare in the very presence of the enemy that I am and will be whatever God has chosen me to be. Why do I stress this? Because *you and I will never impact our world for God until we allow Him to define who we are.* I am not speaking about self-esteem, but rather an understanding of His purpose for our lives. Rest assured, our God will always define you *up*, never down. He will never criticize, slander, humiliate, downgrade or, as my kids used to say, "trash talk" you.

And He will never anoint your past as the prophet of your future. Instead, God will speak wonderful, encouraging and exciting things over you. He says, "You will one day *become*. . . ."

Guard Well Who Speaks into Your Life

I am very selective about whom I allow to speak into my life. Many people can and do speak *to* me, but only I can let down the drawbridge and receive those who speak *into* my life. Solomon warned: "Do not take to heart everything people say" (Ecclesiastes 7:21). And one of his proverbs explains: "Death and life are in the power of the tongue, and those who love it will eat its fruit" (Proverbs 18:21). People who speak *into* our lives are allowed to counsel, influence, guide and have a part in our decision-making. People who speak into our lives have power.

This matters tremendously when it comes to embracing the view through the windshield. As you follow Christ out of the past and into your future, it is very wise to surround yourself with those who define you "up," those who believe about you what God does.

When I was first starting out in ministry, I was not long out of a difficult past. As I said earlier, I received Christ while in a juvenile detention center at sixteen years of age. It would have been easy for me to cast my anchor into the waters of the past, but God brought an older couple my way who became incredible encouragers to me. I was never once with them that they did not speak words of encouragement and hope. I cannot tell you how many times I was downcast, only to be picked up by the "jump-start" words of my friends. They always defined me "up" by talking about God's calling and purpose over my life.

Choose carefully whom you anoint with "speak into" influence in your life. That includes, as we talked about earlier, what you watch, listen to and read. It is easy to tell what kind of person or "voice" you have been around. If you walk away feeling down, discouraged, doubtful, fearful or as though you cannot possibly achieve your dreams, close the drawbridge to your heart. Do not bequeath "speak into" power to those who abuse it. If, on the other hand, you walk away feeling encouraged, hopeful, joyful, full of faith and believing that you can accomplish what God has put on your heart, lower the drawbridge and keep those folks *real close*. Remember, David advised not to walk "in the counsel of the ungodly" (Psalm 1:1).

Why does the enemy try so hard to define you "down"? As we have already seen, he knows that the moment you believe and accept what God says about you, his kingdom is going to receive some damage. Listen to just a few of the things God says about you. As you read, personalize these verses by placing your name in them. *Believe* what God says about you.

- "I can do everything God asks me to with the help of Christ who gives me the strength and power" (Philippians 4:13, TLB).
- "I am sure that God who began the good work within you will keep right on helping you grow in his grace until his task within you is finally finished on that day when Jesus Christ returns" (Philippians 1:6, TLB).
- "The people who know their God shall be strong, and carry out great exploits" (Daniel 11:32).
- "Jesus said to him, 'If you can believe, all things are possible to him who believes'" (Mark 9:23).
- "No eye has seen, no ear has heard, no mind has conceived what God has prepared for those who love him" (1 Corinthians 2:9, NIV).
- "He who believes in Me, the works that I do he will do also; and greater works than these he will do, because I go to My Father" (John 14:12).
- "Yet in all these things we are more than conquerors through Him who loved us" (Romans 8:37).
- "But when the Holy Spirit has come upon you, you will receive power to testify about me with great effect, to the people in Jerusalem, throughout Judea, in Samaria, and to the ends of the earth" (Acts 1:8, TLB).

Get the idea? Alone, your greatest potential is just that—*potential.* On the other hand, in and through Him your greatest potential is realized. The disciples eventually saw this, as did Moses, Abraham, Gideon, the prophets and every other major and minor player in Scripture. This is what waits on the other side of your crossings. This is what emerges once He has defined you.

If you are going to be a witness for Him, you have a bull's-eye painted on your chest *right now.*

Bummer of a Birthmark!

One of my favorite cards to send to fellow ministers shows a classic cartoon by Gary Trudeau, author of *The Far Side*. You may have seen it. It depicts two deer standing in a forest having a talk. One of them has a bull's-eye clearly visible on his chest. The other deer looks at his friend and exclaims, "Bummer of a birthmark, Hal!" Every time I see it I smile, because it is so true of every Christian. If you are going to be a witness for Him, you have a bull's-eye painted on your chest *right now.*

One day, Jesus issued a stern warning to His most promising disciple. "Simon, Simon, Satan has asked to have you, to sift you like wheat, but I have pleaded in prayer for you that your faith should not completely fail" (Luke 22:31–32, TLB). Strong's *Concordance* explains that the word *sift* as used in the New Testament means "to shake in a sieve. Figuratively speaking, by inward agitation to try one's faith to the verge of overthrow." So in other words, *sifting* refers to a trial so strong that the very foundation of our faith is shaken. Christ was informing Peter that his faith was about to be sorely tried. It was not a wonderful "word" from the Lord in the short run, but it was, *oh*, so true.

Why in the world was Satan out to get Simon Peter on such a level? Why was the enemy concerned enough to go directly to God about him as he had with Job? (Read Job 1:6–12.) *Satan wanted to thwart Simon's purpose*; and in thwarting his purpose, he could *redefine* him as a failure and a has-been. The thief was after the word Jesus had spoken over Peter's life. As long as Peter kept on following Jesus, his God-given gifts and abilities would soon be touched by the Holy Spirit at Pentecost and bring great destruction to the devil's kingdom. Consider, for example, a few accounts from Peter's life *after* the sifting of his faith.

- "Then Peter stepped forward with the eleven apostles, and shouted to the crowd, 'Listen, all of you. . . .' And they said to him and to the other apostles, 'Brothers, what should we do?' . . . And those who believed Peter were baptized—about 3,000 in all" (Acts 2:14, 37, 41, TLB). As I have noted before, Peter's first sermon, which lasted three minutes, ushered three thousand souls into the Kingdom of God.
- "Sick people were brought out into the streets on beds and mats so that at least Peter's shadow would fall across some of them as he went by! And crowds came in from the Jerusalem suburbs, bringing their sick folk and those possessed by demons; and every one of them was healed" (Acts 5:15–16, TLB).
- "The night before he was to be executed, he was asleep, double-chained between two soldiers with others standing guard before the prison gate, when suddenly there was a light in the cell and an angel of the Lord stood beside Peter!" (Acts 12:6–7, TLB). Peter was subsequently delivered from prison by an angel in answer to the fervent prayers of the Church: "When [the young girl at the door] recognized Peter's voice, she was so overjoyed that she ran back inside to tell everyone that Peter was standing outside in the street." Some of the disciples replied to her, "It must be his angel." They were wrong. "When they finally went out and opened the door, their surprise knew no bounds" (see verses 14–16, TLB). This was a miraculous intervention of God that brought great encouragement to a young, persecuted Church.

Are we on hell's hit list? If you have yielded your life to Jesus Christ, and have made yourself available to serve Him on any level, the answer is yes!

In short, Peter's "post-sifting" life was marked by thousands of people coming to Christ through his preaching. The sick were healed by his very shadow, and the Church-at-large experienced tremendous encouragement through the supernatural breakthroughs he enjoyed. This is exactly what the enemy wanted to stop. All of this began when Jesus spoke into the life of a crusty fisherman and said, "You will one day *become*. . . ."

We know some of what the enemy attempted to sabotage in Peter's life, but what about our own lives? Is the enemy out to attack us with the same ferocity? Are we on hell's hit list? *If you have yielded your life to Jesus Christ, and have made yourself available to serve Him on any level, the answer is yes!* The formerly fallen and restored Simon Peter warned solemnly,

> Be careful—watch out for attacks from Satan, your great enemy. He prowls around like a hungry, roaring lion, looking for some victim to tear apart. Stand firm when he attacks. Trust the Lord; and remember that other Christians all around the world are going through these sufferings too.
>
> 1 Peter 5:8–9, TLB

According to John's gospel, Satan cannot wrench us from God's hands (see John 10:28–29). Then what is he after by attacking us? The very same thing he was after with Peter. *He wants to hinder, distract and thwart our destiny.* A sold-out, committed Christian, who is dedicated to following Christ, will produce what the serpent fears most. The list below is not exhaustive. Keep in mind as you read that these are just some of the benefits and rewards that wait on the other side of your crossing. They are what Satan does his wicked best to keep you from and are the reason he fights so hard to chain you to the past. A committed, sanctified, totally devoted child of God will produce:

1. Fruit that glorifies God. "It is to the glory of my Father that you should bear much fruit" (John 15:8, JB).
2. Souls won to Christ. "Therefore go and make disciples of all nations" (Matthew 28:19, NIV).
3. A life lived out in the will of God rather than in sin. "I have fought the good fight, I have finished the race, I have kept the faith" (2 Timothy 4:7).
4. Eternal rewards. "If what he [the Christian] has built survives, he will receive his reward" (1 Corinthians 3:14, NIV).
5. The spread of spiritual truth. "His intent was that now, *through the church*, the manifold wisdom of God should be made known to the rulers and authorities in the heavenly realms" (Ephesians 3:10, NIV, emphasis added).
6. God's praises in the earth. "But you are a chosen people, a royal priesthood, a holy nation, a people belonging to God, *that you may declare the praises of him* who called you out of darkness into his wonderful light" (1 Peter 2:9, NIV, emphasis added).

This is a mere sampling of what awaits every believer who gets into the boat and makes the journey from one shore to the next. In your crossings you *become*. When Simon Peter first cast his gaze on the carpenter from Nazareth, do you think he could have ever imagined himself standing before thousands of people from around the world to preach a brand-new Gospel of liberty? If you had told him that one day the sick and dying would line the streets of Jerusalem in hopes that his passing shadow might cast its healing touch over them, do you think he would have believed you? Would the salty fisherman from Galilee have believed that his writings would appear in the Holy Bible and speak to countless millions throughout all time? The answer to each question is a resounding *no* . . . but that's the beauty of it all. To encounter Christ is to come face-to-face with not only your Savior but also your destiny. Part of the package is for your greatest potential to be realized through Him.

I suppose I am a sucker for hope. I just cannot live without it. Recently, I passed through the most difficult trial of my entire life, bar none. In fact, I am writing this book on the other side of what could be best described as a spiritual train wreck. Believe me, it is good to see the sun again. I thought those clouds would never part. I remember thinking to myself when I was in the middle of it all, *What a nightmare it would be if in all of this, I had no hope of a better day!* You cannot live without water and oxygen, and you cannot live without hope. I have, therefore, dedicated the final chapter to singing hope's praises. Won't you join me?

Points to Ponder

1. As you read about the subject of defining, were you able to see who or what your ultimate definer is? If so, was it positive? Negative? If negative, what do you plan to do about it?
2. How important is it to you to experience your greatest potential? Can you identify ways in which God has attempted to bring that about? Elaborate.

True Treasure

> "Again, the kingdom of heaven is like treasure hidden in a field. . . ."
>
> Matthew 13:44

> Anybody who thinks money is everything has never been sick. Or is.
>
> Malcolm S. Forbes

Everyone has a treasure. There is not a person alive who has not stored something as the treasure of his or her heart and prioritized time and attention around it. The Bible says that Jesus "knew all men" (John 2:24). Nothing was hidden from the penetrating eyes of Christ, and He taught that we all harbor a core treasure: "For where your treasure is, there your heart will be also" (Matthew 6:21). Notice, He did not say "where your treasure might be" or "where your treasure will be some day." He said, "For where your treasure is." We all have a treasure *right now.* The things we treasure influence everything we do: The goals we set, the paths we choose, our worldview, the friends we make—all are touched by what we treasure.

> The things we treasure influence everything we do: The goals we set, the paths we choose, our world-view, the friends we make—all are touched by what we treasure.

What Makes Something a Treasure?

To better illustrate the concept of treasure, let's pretend that each of us has one hundred tokens at our disposal. Each token represents an emotional investment that we are free to place in anything we choose. I might, for instance, place three tokens into a casual friendship. If the friendship fails, there is little pain or regret. After all, it was only three tokens. I might be hard at work earning a college degree. A lot more is riding on this pursuit, let's say thirty tokens. Much of my future success, security and happiness hinges on reaching this goal. In the end, I will have invested hundreds of hours of work, which means my investment is significant. If for some reason I fail or lose my college funding and cannot finish the program, the emotional hurt would be felt deeply.

Even thirty tokens, however, do not a treasure make. True treasure demands far more. You know that someone or something has taken on true treasure status when you invest all one hundred tokens at once. True treasure puts everything on the line. Jesus required such "all or nothing" devotion: "He who loves father or mother more than Me is not worthy of Me. And he who loves son or daughter more than Me is not worthy of Me" (Matthew 10:37). Truly following Jesus requires all of your tokens!

You might be wondering what this has to do with the windshield and the rearview mirror. Remember, Jesus urged us to recall Lot's wife. Just when God was opening up an exciting new future (seen through the windshield), she was unable to tear herself away from the sights in the rearview mirror. All of her emotional tokens were still in Sodom. This is why the Bible warns: "Keep your heart with all diligence, for out of it spring the issues of life" (Proverbs 4:23). Beware what you give your whole heart to, for once you cross that line the investment level is huge, and it is difficult to pull away. The greatest reason of all for turning from the rearview mirror to the windshield ahead is the treasure of knowing Christ.

Core Treasures, Core Pursuits

Your *core treasure* will produce a *core pursuit*. A core pursuit is what you give the best of your strength, talent and time to obtain. It becomes the central focus of your life, your primary drive. We could safely paraphrase Matthew 6:21 as: "Whatever your treasure is, that is what you will pursue." Watch what a person pursues above all else and you will know the chief treasure of his or her heart. Where your treasure is, there your heart will be. And where your heart is, there your feet will follow. God is concerned about our core pursuits and speaks to this issue repeatedly in His Word. Here are just a few examples:

> "Pursue love, and desire spiritual gifts" (1 Corinthians 14:1).
>
> "But you, O man of God, flee these things and pursue righteousness, godliness, faith, love, patience, gentleness" (1 Timothy 6:11).
>
> "He who would love life and see good days . . . let him seek peace and pursue it" (1 Peter 3:10–11).

Look at the list of virtues we are commanded to crown as core pursuits: *love, righteousness, godliness, faith, patience, gentleness and peace*. Now I ask you, how many people do you

> Your core pursuit is the spiritual stethoscope that reveals your soul's delight.

know who could honestly say these character qualities are on their "top ten list" of things to pursue?

Your core pursuit is the spiritual stethoscope that reveals your soul's delight. Core pursuits show whether or not God has successfully captured your heart. "So they come to you as people do, they sit before you as My people, and they hear your words, but they do not do them; for with their mouth they show much love, *but their hearts pursue their own gain*" (Ezekiel 33:31, emphasis added). Obviously, God knows what our core pursuits are, no matter what they look like on the outside. What is your core pursuit? God? Money? Fame? The approval of others?

Not only does your core pursuit provide a reading on the heartbeat of your soul, it also spawns all other pursuits. As goes your core pursuit, so go all secondary pursuits. For centuries it was believed that the earth was the center of our solar system. All other planets, it was thought, revolved around it. The Church of the Middle Ages believed this so strongly that anyone who taught otherwise was considered a heretic and either imprisoned or martyred! The Church was, of course, wrong. The sun is the center of our solar system and all the planets revolve around it. This fact of creation provides a perfect picture of how core pursuits work: All of your secondary pursuits revolve around your core pursuit. Finances, relationships, self-control, happiness, fulfillment; everything is affected by it.

This is why Jesus left clear instructions on what our primary pursuit must be: "But seek first the kingdom of God and His righteousness" (Matthew 6:33). Can you see Jesus' number one priority? We are not forbidden to pursue other things; it simply means that, just as rain follows clouds, so all other pursuits flow out of whatever our core pursuit happens to be. If your core pursuit is the Kingdom of God, which for me is summed up in Christ, you can rest assured that all other pursuits will be worthy and beneficial. If your core pursuit is worldly, fleshly or carnal, watch out! All other pursuits will bow down to serve it.

Paul's Pursuit

Paul was transparent about the treasures/pursuits that fueled his highly productive life. Before we look into this further, keep in mind that the great apostle advised us to follow his example: "For you yourselves know how it is necessary to imitate our example. . . . [We wished] to make ourselves an example for you to follow" (2 Thessalonians 3:7, 9, AMP).

Now, look at this description of one of his pursuits that he expected us to follow: "Not that I have already obtained all this, or have already been made perfect, but I press on to take hold of *that* for which Christ Jesus took hold of me" (Philippians 3:12, NIV, emphasis added).

What was the "that" that Paul was pressing on to take hold of? Just before his martyrdom, he wrote this to Timothy: "I have fought a good fight, I have finished my course, I have kept the faith" (2 Timothy 4:7, KJV). Note the words *my course*. As his final days grew near, Paul was confident that he had fulfilled his own unique purpose—that for which the Lord had apprehended him. I am convinced by Scripture and experience that we all have a "that," a purpose for which God has called us. To miss it is to miss the true meaning and purpose of life. No wonder Jesus warned: "What gain, then, is it for a man to have won the whole world and to have lost or ruined his very self?" (Luke 9:25, JB).

It may be that, like Paul, your mission is "in the spotlight," perhaps preaching to a large congregation. Or maybe your "that" finds its fulfillment "backstage" where you are a steady witness to the people you work with, demonstrating your faith in day-to-day life. You might be called to teach, work with children or show acts of kindness to your neighbors. Whatever God has called you to do, remember Jesus' command to every believer throughout the ages: "Let your light so shine before men, that they may see your good works and glorify your Father in heaven" (Matthew 5:16). It is up to every individual who follows Him to find his or her own unique way to let these lights shine.

In whatever way your "that" manifests, know that—to quote another apostle—we are all called to "proclaim the praises of Him who called [us] out of darkness into His marvelous light" (1 Peter 2:9). Notice that He calls us "out of" something so that He might call us "into" something new. Each time I arise and obediently follow Jesus to the next destination, I discover another glimmer of light that can be used for His glory. When our core pursuit is the Kingdom of God (which is Christ), then "that" for which we were apprehended becomes clear.

The Greatest Treasure of All

Tucked away between Ecclesiastes and Isaiah is the beautiful little poetic book called the Song of Solomon. Two main characters emerge in the drama that unfolds: the "Shulamite," who represents the Church, and the "Beloved," who represents Christ. In the opening verses we find the Shulamite (the Church) asking the Beloved (Christ) to "Draw me away!" (1:4). The Beloved responds a bit later by saying, "Rise up, my love, my fair one, and come away!" (2:13).

I hear an echo of "Let us cross over to the other side" in those words. Jesus is ever calling us onward, and we are to ever follow after Him. Throughout Solomon's Song, the Shulamite is in pursuit of the Beloved. This is the dance of discipleship. The greatest reward of all—far above reaching our sea of faces, realizing our maximum potential or fulfilling that for which we were apprehended—is the inexpressible joy of progressively coming to know Him.

What is it that yanks at the strings of our hearts and bids us pull up the tent pegs, don our backpacks and set out on yet another venture of faith? I will tell you truthfully, if it were merely for the sake of a set of religious rules and regulations, I would be the first one to bail out. If it were merely for religion's sake, I would probably chuck the whole thing and become a self-serving man tomorrow. But I know that is not what it is all about. Jesus has captured my heart. I hear Him ever saying, *Rise up, my love, my fair one, and come away.* True spiritual health is measured by our pursuit of Him, not by how many times in a given week we attend Church or by how many Christian bumper stickers adorn our cars.

When you think about it, this thing called Christianity does not fit into the category of the logical. Having never seen, touched or walked beside Him as the disciples did, we love Jesus Christ! Not perfectly, but truly. This walk is not the love of an "idea" or the glorification of a "good person." Those things cannot keep us going. A love affair began the moment the love of God was "poured out in our hearts by the Holy Spirit who was given to us" (Romans 5:5). Peter told his readers, "You love him even though you have never seen him; though not seeing him, you trust him" (1 Peter 1:8, TLB).

What do you think compelled Simon Peter to leave hearth and home to follow Christ? Was it only to become all that God had destined for him? Not ultimately. He wanted Christ. His heart had been captured. Likewise, what could possibly have driven Paul to risk life and limb, endlessly enduring the laundry list of troubles that befell him in his ministry labors? (See 2 Corinthians 11:24–28.) He did not leave us wondering. As he tells us,

In short, if making the effort to leave the past behind will enrich our relationship with Christ, that in itself is the greatest reward of all.

> Yes, everything else is worthless when compared with the priceless gain of knowing Christ Jesus my Lord. I have put aside all else, counting it worth less than nothing, in order that I can have Christ, and become one with him.
>
> Philippians 3:8–9, TLB

Paul's story would be an enigma wrapped up in a mystery apart from this one fact: Jesus had captured his heart.

Each time the great apostle stood up following a brutal beating, he measured pain against reward and said, "I believe nothing can happen that will outweigh the supreme advantage of knowing Christ Jesus my Lord" (Philippians 3:8, JB). When he walked long and lonely miles to carry the precious Gospel to yet another town or people, it was not the thrill of preaching that drove him, nor was it some egotistical desire to be great. He told us his motive: "All I want is to know Christ and to experience the power of his resurrection" (Philippians 3:10, JB). His treasure was Christ, and his feet followed in hot pursuit. It is why he was always crossing to the other side of "somewhere" in his journey of faith. In short, if making the effort to leave the past behind will enrich our relationship with Christ, that in itself is the greatest reward of all.

Prisoners of Hope

I have a confession to make. I am a prisoner of hope. I did not always know this the way I do now. It took some deep valleys, harsh trials, fiery ovens and long seasons of groping in the dark to reveal that I am a "hope junkie" at heart. There were times I wished it were not so, times when hope seemed almost to be a foe. Hope can actually bring a certain frustration when you really want to let go and fall off the face of the earth—but hope just will not let you do it. In the face of terrible odds, when no one would place his bets on you, hope always does. When you are down for the count and everyone else has walked away, hope doesn't. Hope is a stubborn friend. In Psalm 27:13, David writes about the tenacity of hope: "I would have lost heart, unless I had believed that I would see the goodness of the Lord in the land of the living."

It took some deep valleys, harsh trials, fiery ovens and long seasons of groping in the dark to reveal that I am a "hope junkie" at heart.

When you are in a pit and see no way out, hope whispers, "Wait on the Lord; be of good courage, and He shall strengthen your heart; wait, I say, on the Lord!" (verse 14). "Do not put up the white flag just yet," cries hope. The writer of Hebrews calls hope "an anchor of the soul" (Hebrews 6:19). The anchor that hope drops into the waters of turmoil is its undying belief in the goodness of the Lord. Hope believes that the yet unseen hand of God is working for our good and we will rejoice in His plan when we see it.

Hope is the most hopeful optimist on earth! It keeps us sane and steady in times of trial. When you see someone filled with optimism, bet on it, you can track the source to hope. Optimism is hope's child. Hope looks beyond the darkness of today and sees a brighter tomorrow. It expects the Almighty to intrude into the nightmares of life by turning things around in a way that makes you dance and shout with joy.

I cannot live without hope. I am telling you the truth. I would rather set up shop in a cardboard box on a downtown street corner than live without hope. I cannot fathom a life not graced with the hope of hope! A hopeless life is one of undiluted hell. I suppose this is one of the reasons I am so thankful for the God I serve. He is "the God of hope" (Romans 15:13) and the author of hope, and His presence is the soil that hope grows best in. Then when

The anchor that hope drops into the waters of turmoil is its undying belief in the goodness of the Lord.

hope reaches maturity within us, we find that we have "the full assurance of hope" (Hebrews 6:11, KJV).

The difference between faith and hope, as best I can understand it, is that faith *believes* God while hope *expects* Him. Look at the first verse of the great chapter on faith: "Now faith is the substance of things *hoped* for" (Hebrews 11:1, emphasis added). In this verse we discover faith and hope working side by side to bring about an answer from God. Faith believes the promises and, perhaps more importantly, in the God of the promises. Faith places its full trust in the character and integrity of God. Hope, on the other hand, holds out a happy anticipation that what has been promised is on the way! According to Vine's *Dictionary*, the Greek word for *hope* is defined as "favorable and confident expectation. It has to do with the unseen and the future. Hope describes the happy anticipation of good." Faith believes, while hope expects. Hand-in-hand they are invaluable tools for every Christian, leading us like a faithful compass through the storms and uncertainties of life.

As goes faith, so goes hope. You might say that faith is the foundation that hope builds its house upon. If hope dies, you can bet that faith dwindled first—because again, hope expects what faith believes. If hope is gone, the diagnosis has to be that faith has stopped believing God. This is why it is so crucial to feed your faith: "So then faith cometh by hearing, and hearing by the word of God" (Romans 10:17, KJV).

Bible hope is utterly trustworthy, of course, for it is established on the eternal God. Because of who He is we have "mighty indwelling strength and strong encouragement to grasp and hold fast *the hope appointed for us and set before* [*us*]" (Hebrews 6:18, AMP, emphasis added).

Why this little teaching about hope and faith? As you break the shackles of the past, turn toward the future God has laid out before you and step forward boldly, crowning Him your greatest treasure, you must be sure to take faith in one hand and hope in the other. Oh, and do not forget to put perseverance in your backpack. You will never reach the other side without their help. In fact, you must become a willing "prisoner of hope" to arrive safely at your next destination.

As you break the shackles of the past, turn toward the future God has laid out before you and step forward boldly, you must be sure to take faith in one hand and hope in the other.

Look at these words of Zechariah: "As for you also, because of the blood of your covenant, I will set your prisoners free from the waterless pit. Return to the stronghold, you prisoners of hope. Even today I declare that I will restore double to you" (Zechariah 9:11-12).

Oh, and do not forget to put perseverance in your backpack.

Zechariah's ministry took place during the time of Israel's release from Babylonian captivity. For a dozen years or so the task of rebuilding the Temple, which was destroyed when the Jewish people were taken captive, had been half completed. Zechariah was called by God to encourage the people to return to the work. Rather than rebuke them for their weakening zeal, the prophet encouraged them with visions of a glorious future. The Temple had to be built, for one day the Messiah's glory would inhabit it! They were not just building a building; they were building their future.

Paradoxically, Zechariah said that two things imprisoned the people. The first was that they were prisoners of a waterless pit. This waterless pit was probably a metaphor for the horrible captivity they had experienced for seventy grueling years. Figuratively speaking, it represented a complete lack of spiritual sustenance. It felt as though they were dying of spiritual thirst. They had no sense of the flow of blessing.

I have learned that any place God has not led me invariably winds up being a pit with no water. The flow of spiritual

The flow of spiritual water is found only in the center of God's will.

water is found only in the center of God's will. As Jesus told the woman at the well,

> Every one who drinks of this water will thirst again, but whoever drinks of the water that I shall give him will never thirst; the water that I shall give him will become in him a spring of water welling up to eternal life.
>
> John 4:13–14, RSV

Can you see that the past, if we linger there too long, is a pit with no water? Just ask anybody who desperately needs deliverance from the shackles of trauma, heartbreak, bitterness, failure, past successes or inordinate attachments if a flow of God's blessing exists there! In fact, these bondages to the past are best described as imprisonment. The "six chains" we discussed in Part 1 are prisons of the soul, and that is where hope comes in. The children of Israel were in a pit with no water, yet they could not shake the voice of hope. Thomas Fuller rightly said, "If it were not for hopes, the heart would break."

Do you see the second prison indicated in Zechariah's words? The Israelites were also prisoners of hope, which held them with velvet chains. Why? Because God had promised to be with His people "because of the blood of your covenant" (9:11). You, like them, are not coming out of captivity based on your merits: It can be done only by and through the New Covenant blood of the Lamb. God has made a blood covenant with you through Christ, and there is absolutely nothing stronger in all of Scripture than a blood covenant.

> Now may the God of peace who brought up our Lord Jesus from the dead, that great Shepherd of the sheep, through the blood of the everlasting covenant, make you complete in every

> good work to do His will, working in you what is well pleasing in His sight.
>
> Hebrews 13:20–21

The journey may not be an easy one. That is why we must become prisoners of hope.

The prophet Zechariah then told the people: "Return to the stronghold" (9:12). What is the stronghold we are to turn to when leaving the captivity of the past? Our stronghold is Christ! He is our keeper in the day of battle, our "stronghold" in the hour of trouble. Let me speak to you right where you are. All that you really need to cross to the other side is Christ. The book of Colossians tells us that in Him dwells "all the fullness of the Godhead bodily" (2:9). It adds that "in [Him] are hidden all the treasures of wisdom and knowledge" (2:3). He is all-sufficient!

Whenever we find ourselves in some type of captivity, the voice of the Bridegroom can be heard saying, *Rise up, my love, my fair one, and come away*. The desire to become what He has destined us to be, along with the knowledge that others will benefit from our struggles, only fuels our motivation. And the longing to know Him tugs at the deepest level of our hearts. But we have seen that the journey may not be an easy one—sudden storms and frustrating winds can dampen our zeal. That is why we must become prisoners of hope.

The same Lord who carried the disciples safely across the perilous sea will also carry you from where you are to where you need to be. As you pursue Him, He will cause you to become exactly what He has called you to be. The Lord of glory will guide you into apprehending that for which He apprehended you. He will see to it that you reach those who are part of your destiny. And best of all, He will gently carry you into an ever-growing, ever-deepening relationship with Him. He is the object upon which our hope is marvelously fixed (see 1 Timothy 1:1).

Wait a moment. Do you see those faces in the distance? Look at their expressions. They have been waiting for you to arrive! And by the way, have you noticed how much stronger you have become since you turned your gaze from the rearview mirror? God knew that would happen. It is what He has desired for you . . . and as you have journeyed, I can only imagine what you have learned about Christ, the greatest Treasure of all. Isn't He worth all the trouble of leaving the past behind? Isn't He more to be desired than gold? Keep pursuing Him with all your might—your eyes focused ahead, steady and hopeful. He is worth every effort, all the pain, all the inconveniences along the way. As you pursue Him, you will continue to become all that He has destined you to be.

I'll leave you now. I have some journeying of my own to do. Perhaps I'll see you on the other side!

Born in upstate New York, **Jeff Wickwire** grew up in Dallas, Texas, after moving with his family at five years of age. At sixteen, after being arrested for drug involvement at the height of the "hippie" movement, Jeff experienced a dynamic conversion to Christ.

Since then Jeff has served in many capacities, including prison minister, youth pastor, college and career director, radio evangelist and, for the last 22 years, senior pastor.

Jeff graduated from the University of North Texas and continued his education at Luther Rice Seminary and Tyndale Theological Seminary, where he earned both his master's and doctoral degrees.

Jeff has founded three successful, growing churches. He currently serves as pastor of Turning Point Fellowship in Fort Worth. One of the earmarks of Jeff's ministry has been large numbers of conversions. Thousands of people have been won to Christ through the years.

Jeff is known for his practical, clear and timely messages that "put something in your pocket you can carry home and use the next day." His vivid illustrations and common-sense approach to Scripture are widely known for making Christianity easy to understand and live.

Jeff currently lives in Fort Worth with his wife, Cathy.

Jeff has written *Making It Right When You Feel Wronged* (Chosen, 2003) and *Gossip, Slander and Other Favorite Pastimes* (Turning Point, 2005).

For booking and/or product information please contact:

Dr. Jeff Wickwire
P.O. Box 161069
Fort Worth, TX 76161
Email: wickjl@sbcglobal.net